POCKET LIBRARY OF "STUDIES" IN ART
V

ALDO NEPPI MODONA

A GUIDE

TO

ETRUSCAN ANTIQUITIES

With 36 illustrations
and a touristic map

LEO S. OLSCHKI EDITORE

FIRENZE

MCMLXVIII

English Translation by Andrew Page
Sixth Edition, revised by the Author

———

All rights reserved
Copyright by Leo S. Olschki - *Florence*

———

Printed by Tipolitografia F.lli Linari - Florence

36762

SELECTED BIBLIOGRAPHY

L. Banti, *Il mondo degli Etruschi* (Rome, 1960).

G. Buonamici, *Epigrafia etrusca* (Florence 1935).

G. Dennis, *The Cities and Cemeteries of Etruria,* 2 vols. (4th Edition in « Everyman's Library », London, 1907).

P. Ducati, *Etruria Antica*, 2 vols. (2nd Edition, Turin, 1927).

— *Storia dell'Arte Etrusca*, 2 vols. (Florence, 1927).

G. Q. Giglioli, *L'Arte Etrusca* (Milan, 1933).

G. M. Mansuelli, *Etruria* (Milano, 1963).

B. Nogara, *Gli Etruschi e la loro civiltà* (Milan, 1933).

M. Pallottino, *Etruscologia*, 5ª ed. (Milano, 1962).

PREFACE

The rapidity with which the preceeding editions (two Italian, two English and one Franch) have sold out, bears testimony on the one hand to the favour with which this book has been received by the Italian and foreign public, and on the other hand to the ever growing interest of other countries in the Etruscan civilization. Therefore it depends on the considerable results of the materials discovered, eventually studied and published, not to mention the greater general knowledge obtained by means of the various exhibitions in the many European countries.

The chief merit of this little book is its brevity, maintaining it at all costs, although there would have been so much to say on general matters. For the reader who requires further knowledge, I would refer him to the essential bibliography which preceedes this preface.

The other merit of this guide is the itineries which have always been much appreciated: now for the first time it has been entirely transformed, giving notice of the main highways rather than the railways, assuming that most tourists by now use the former. The other innovation is to indicate in a short appendix, the places where the ruins are least accessible or are of little interest.

As is natural in a short practical book of this kind, I have omitted any critical discussion of the various problems, which have on occurrence, been simply pointed out. As yet I have omitted any footnotes of bibliographic quotations.

A. N. M.

A GUIDE
TO
ETRUSCAN ANTIQUITIES

I

TOPOGAPHICAL TOURIST GUIDE

ANSEDONIA (Cosa) Ruins. (Grosseto, Orbetello).

It is reached by taking the road Aurelia (S.S. n. 1) and turning on to a by-road (at 137,7 kms) which leads to a farm house. From there it is a 20 minute walk to the top of a hill jutting out over the sea. Probably the old port of Vulci (32 kms).

Considerable parts of the encircling walls (Roman) and towers well preserved, numerous Roman ruins near the city. Below is the *Tagliata Etrusca,* or outlet of Lake Burano, and the impressive, well known grotto called *Bagno* or *Spacco della Regina*, together with the ruins of *Sub- cosa* (?). This site is reached by descending (on foot) from the ruins of *Cosa* or by a road which turns off the Aurelia road a little after the turning for Cosa, with a level crossing at signal box no. 143.

AREZZO (Arretium).

Remains of the walls outside the city near the fortress and elsewhere, and near the church of S. Cornelio on the hill of the same name (also called Castelsecco outside Porta Trieste).

Archaeological museum « Mecenate » in the ex-convent of S. Bernardo (Via Margaritone), with objects in « bucchero », bronzes, urns, Aretine vases etc.

ARTIMINO (Firenze, Carmignano). Turn off the S.S. n. 67 at Lastra a Signa, or from Poggio a Caiano off the S.S. n. 66 taking the road for Carmignano (5 kms), and from there to Artimino (6,3 kms).

Burial tumuli between the Villa Artimino and the grounds of the Grumolo farm and the Podere Grumaggio.

Etruscan antiquities incorporated into the facade of the Pieve (parish church), and also inside.

ASCIANO (Siena). Turn off the S.S. n. 73 at Arbia (7,2 kms from Siena), or off the S.S. n. 2 at Buonconvento making for Rapolano.

At 4 kms the necropolis of Poggio Pinci with sepulchres, (4th - 1st century B.C.).

Small civic museum in the church of San Bernardino (apply to the Palazzo Municipale).

BARBANO ROMANO (*Manturanum?*) (Viterbo). Turn off the S.S. n. 2 at 45,6 kms (Manziana) along the road from Vetralla as far as Veiano (6 kms). From there take the road to the left before the bridge onto the road for B.R. (2 kms).

Necropolis of S. Giuliano.

BARBERINO DI VAL D'ELSA (Firenze). On the S.S. n. 2, between Firenze and Poggibonsi.

Alabaster urns and pottery at the Municipio (town hall), discovered in tombs in the vicinity; one is at S. Martino ai Colli.

BIEDA

BISENZIO (Visentium). Ruins. (Rome, Capodimonte). On a hill on the west side of the Lake Bolsena, near the by-road Capodimonte-Valentano. Rejoined by a slope that branches off at the Capella di S. Agabito on the road that completes the way round Lake Bolsena. Reached by the S.S. n. 2 turning off at Bolsena, or by the S.S. n. 74 turning off between Gràdoli and Làtera at 77,9 kms.

Ruins and tombs.

BLERA (formerly *Bieda*). (Viterbo). From Viterbo on the S.S. n. 2 (Cassia). Continue for 8 kms after Vetrella, turning off in the vicinity of « La Cura ».

Necropolis on the other side of the Rio Canale, with rock tombs with architectural facades.

At about 1 km from Blera on the by-road, an Etruscan bridge over the Biedano stream, along which are Etruscan tombs and remains of Etruscan walls.

BOLSENA (Volsinium, Volsini). (Viterbo). 18 kms from Montefiascone and 30 kms from Viterbo on the S.S. n. 2 (Cassia) at 120 kms from Siena. Civic antiquarium on the ground floor of the Palazzo Municipio. Small archaeological collection in the rectory of the S. Cristina church. Tombs, walls and a temple in the neighbourhood.

BOMARZO (Polimartium). (Viterbo). Turn off the S.S. n. 204 (Viterbo-Orte), at 3,1 kms, 3,5 kms from the turning off from the S.S. n. 204 (Viterbo-Orte).

An Etruscan collection in the Palazzo Orsini.

Remains of walls, drains and tombs at Piano della Colonna, about 3 kms N. W., beyond the stream Vezza; (more easily reached from Sipicciano station on the Viterbo-Orte line). Of interest is the *Grotta dipinta* and the *Grotta della Colonna.*

CAERE. See *CERVÉTERI*

CAMPIGLIA MARITTIMA (Livorno). Turn off the S.S. n. 1 (Aurelia) at Venturina at 89,2 kms (4,6 kms).

Etruscan kilns at *Madonna di Fucinaia.* In the town, a small collection owned by the Del Mancino family.

CANINO (Viterbo). Turn off the S.S. n. 1 (Aurelia) at Montalto di Castro; along the road from Valentano at 19 kms.

Civic museum with Etruscan objects.

CAPENA (formerly Leprignano). Turn off the S.S. n. 3 (Flaminia) near Morlupo station (8,3 kms).

Remains of tombs especially at Monte Tufello, the contents of which are in the Villa Giulia museum, Rome.

The old centre of Capena was perhaps 3 kms towards the N.E., in the locality of Civitùcola.

CASALE MARITTIMO (Pisa). Turn off the S.S. n. 1 (Aurelia) at Cecina (14 kms).

It is easy to find the place of the tomb which has been reconstructed in the grounds of the Archaeological Museum in Firenze.

S.E. from the centre, at Castelvecchio, on a small hill, are preserved the remains of a farm of the late Etrusco-Roman era.

Objects in the Antiquarium of Cecina.

CASINO DI TERRA (Pisa, Guardistallo). Turn off the S.S. n. 1 (Aurelia) near Cecina at S. Pietro in Palazzo.

Near the station, remains of a tomb called *Casaglia,* with objects in the Cancellieri farm.

CASTEL D'ASSO (Castellanum Axia) Ruins. (Viterbo). 8,5 kms west of Viterbo leaving by Porta Faul.

Remains of walls, drains and a gate. Necropolis in the Valle del Fosso Procoio, on the right of the stream Arcione, with about 30 tombs excavated out of the tufa, with architectural facades and inscriptions.

CASTELLINA IN CHIANTI (Siena). Turn off the S.S. n. 2 at Siena or Poggibonsi, or directly along the Chiantigiana road from Firenze (48,5), or from Siena (21,3).

Archaic hypogeum at Montecalvario.

CASTIGLIONCELLO (Livorno, Rosignano Marittimo). On the S.S. n. 1 (Aurelia) between Cecina and Livorno.

Small Archaeological museum of Etruscan antiquities from the tombs in the neighbourhood, on the Poggetto at the top of the Via del Porto. (Apply to the Azienda Autonoma del Turismo). Also ruins of the necropolis in the Rosignano Alto museum.

CASTIGLIONE DEL LAGO (Perugia). On the S.S. n. 71, at 195 kms from Rome.

Small civic collection of Etruscan antiquities in the Municipio (town hall), with urns and fragments of pottery.

CASTRO (ruins) - See *FARNESE*.

CÉCINA (Livorno). On the S.S. n. 1 (Aurelia), 34 kms from Livorno.

Antiquarium in the Municipio, with antiquities from the neighbourhood.

CERVÉTERI (Kisria, Caere [vetus]). (Rome). Situated at 3 kms from the turning off the S.S. n. 1 (Aurelia) at 41 kms. Not to be confused with *Ceri (Caere Novum)*, situated a little further to the east, where there is nothing Etruscan, having been founded in the 13th century A.D.

Museum in the fortress of the town.

Remains of walls. A vast necropolis on the *Banditaccia* hill near the village to the north, in the care of the State, (tracks only suitable for motor vehicles in the good season). For the free guide to the site, apply to the Head-Office of the excavations at the end of the lane. There are about ten various burial chambers and tumuli of the greatest interest, with some painted reliefs and inscriptions.

Of great importance is the isolated tomb called « Regolini-Galassi », of very ancient construction and for the precious contents which are now housed in the Gregorian Etruscan museum in the Vatican. It is situated about 1 km from the village beyond the Fossa Vaccina, near the Bracciano road, beneath an isolated building of the farm called « Il Sorbo ». To visit the tomb, apply to the wine shop in the village owned by Pietro Valeri. Some other very interesting tombs are scattered about in the neighbourhood but are not easily accessible. They are the tombs of *Campana* on Monte Abetone (2 kms to the south), the tomb of the *Vestibolo rotondo* on Monte dell'Oro (5 kms to the N.E.), the *Sedia* on Monte Padua; *Torlonia*; several in the Zambra district to the west. See S. SEVERA.

CETONA (Siena). 8 kms from Chiusi goods yard, turning off the S.S. n. 71. (Autostrada del Sole, Chiusi toll-gate).

Private collection of Etruscan antiquities in the Palazzo Terrosi. Prehistoric caves on Monte Cetona near S. Maria di Belvedere. (The contents are housed in the archaeological museum in Perugia).

CHIANCIANO TERME (Siena). S.S. n. 146 from Chiusi (15 kms).

Tombs in the neighbourhood. Inscriptions and sarcophagi in the vestibule of the Chiesa della Collegiata (14 kms).

CHIUSI (Chamars, Clusium) (Siena). On the S.S. n. 71. (Autostrada del Sole).

Remains of walls and underground galleries beneath the Duomo, near the Porta Romana and the Porta al Prato: National Archaeological Museum (Piazza della Cattedrale), where one asks for the guide to the *Tomba della Scimmia*, (5 kms motor road), on the Poggio Renzo, which contains some characteristic scenic paintings, (nearby are other inaccessible tombs). On the road to the *Tomba della Scimmia* (leaving by the Via Porsenna, and continuing in a N.E. direction, but can also be reached from the opposite side by turning off to the right, off the road to Sinalunga), beyond the railway, is the *Tomba del Granduca* or *Paccianese* (custodian in the adjacent cottage). Then, nearer the city in the same direction (on the by-road) is the *Tomba del Colle* (custodian in the adjacent cottage), with its splendid original door and paintings, and the Tomba della Tassinaia. The *Tomba di Vigna Grande,* on a hill to the south of Chiusi, is reached across the fields along a path which turns off to the left at the beginning of the road leading from the station to the city.

Tomb of *Poggio Gaiella* or *Porsenna* (by-road turning off at Dolciano from the Sinalunga road about 5 kms from Chiusi), to the north side near a lake. Very interesting; chambers and galleries one above the other, but the greater part has collapsed.

Other tombs are not easily accessible.

CITTÀ DELLA PIEVE (Perugia). On the S.S. n. 71 (at 43 kms from Orvieto).

Civic museum.

CIVITA CASTELLANA (Falerî Véteres) (Viterbo). On the S.S. n. 3 (Flaminia), 54,4 kms from Rome.

Traces of walls near the viaduct over the Treia, to the S.E. Necropolis between Ponte Terrano and Ponte Clementino, beyond the larger ditch, which is reached by the Roman road (turning to the right).

Another group of tombs about 4 kms away near the Rio del Purgatorio, near the stream of the 'Sassi Rotti' (broken stones), and on the Poggio del Vignale.

Ruins of a temple at Celle. Remains of the temples of Scasato and Sassa Caduti, transferred to the Villa Giulia museum, Rome.

Remains of an acquaduct near Ponte Terreno.

CIVITA LAVINIA

CIVITAVECCHIA (Rome). On the S.S. n. 1 (Aurelia), 72 kms to the north of Rome.

Civic museum near the Largo Plebiscito.

Etruscan sarcophagi.

Etruscan necropolis called *La Scaglia*. Reached by turning off the Aurelia towards the beach at 77 kms.

COLLE DI VAL D'ELSA - See *MONTERIGGIONE*.

COLONNA - See *VETULONIA*.

COMEANA (Firenze, Carmignano).

Turn off to Lastra a Signa, on the S.S. n. 67, or from Poggio a Caiano on the S.S. n. 66, taking the road for Carmignano.

Burial tumuli called *Buschetti,* near the cemetery, and from *Montefortini,* the beginning of the road from Comeana to Signa (excavations in progress).

CORCHIANO (Fescennium?) (Viterbo).

Turn off the S.S. n. 3 (Flaminia) to Civita Castellana by way of Carbognano (13,9 kms) or by the S.S. n. 2 (Cassia) to Viterbo.

Scattered tombs with inscriptions, especially near the bridge over the Rio Fratta (1 km) and at Puntone del Ponte (3 kms) on the road from Vignanello. Remains of drains near the Rio Fratta.

Small private collection of local antiquities owned by the Crescenzi family.

CORNETO - See *TARQUINIA.*

CORTONA (Curtuna) (Arezzo). On the S.S. n. 71, between Arezzo and Terontola.

Remains of domestic buildings and of the encircling walls.

Museum of the Etruscan Academy with the famous bronze lamp, urns, bronzes, coins, etc.

Tombs: *Tanella* or *Grotta di Pitagora* (open; on foot, 5 minutes S. W. of the city, leaving by the Porta S. Vincenzo; by car, turn off the road to the station above the Chiesa del Calcinaio).

Tomba del Sodo, not far from the site of the same name near the main Arezzo road, from which one descends on the by-road from Porta S. Maria (custodian in the adjacent cottage).

Melone di Camucia, near the railway station (entrance through the vineyard above the mill).

Other tombs in the vicinity.

COSA - See *ANSEDONIA.*

FALERII - See *CIVITA CASTELLANA.*

FARNESE (Castro). Ruins. (Viterbo). Turn off the S.S. n. 2 at Bolsena, or near Gràdoli on the S.S. n. 74, then follow the road that turns off at Valentano for Manciano (10,2 kms). [Autostrada del Sole, toll-gate at Orvieto].

Tombs in the neighbourhood, and near the ruins of Castro, 8 kms to the east along the river Olpeta.

FÈRENTO (Ferentium). (Viterbo). Ruins 8 kms from Viterbo [S.S. n. 2 (Cassia)], along the road to Bagnoregio, turning to the right near a school after 8 kms.

Rock-tombs in the neighbourhood.

Remains of the Etrusco-Roman theatre.

FERRARA, MUSEO ARCHEOLOGICO

FIESOLE (Faesulae) (Firenze). A few kms from the centre of the town.

Remains of walls in several villas, and on the acropolis of the monastery of San Francesco; also remains of a small Etruscan and a larger Etrusco-Roman temple, and some tombs.

Fiesole museum (Via Marini) with Etrusco-Roman objects.

FIRENZE *(Florentia)*. [Autostrada del Sole].

Archaeological museum (Via della Colonna, 38) with the Topographical Museum of Etruria; gallery with facsimiles of Etruscan pictures, urns, bronzes, sculpture, gold articles and coins. In the garden: reconstructions of tombs, for the most part with the original materials.

Instituto di Studi Etruschi e Italici, in the same building with the Etruscological library (collections of XXXV volumes of *Etruscan Studies;* Quaderni Etruschi; works on Etruscan civilization; minutes of conventions and congresses; Publications and « Monumenti »; maps of the towns and regions of Etruria; catalogues; inscriptions; etc.).

At the offices of the Superintendent of Etruscan Antiquities (Via della Pergola, 65) on the third floor, is an Etruscological library, open to all students with special permission.

There is a private collection in the Palazzo *Antinori-Aldobrandini* (Via dei Serragli, 7): urns mostly from Volterra with inscriptions.

GROSSETO [S.S. n. 1 (Aurelia)].

Archaeological museum in the Palazzo delle Scuole Classiche (Via Mazzini, 28) in the Chelliana library, (objects from Roselle, cineary urns, also from Vetulonia, vases, buccheri, terracottas etc.).

GROTTE DI CASTRO (Viterbo). Turn off the SS. n. 2 at S. Lorenzo Nuovo (to the north of Lake Bolsena) to Làtera (4,6 kms).

Tombs in the neighbourhood.

GROTTE S. STEFANO (Viterbo). [S.S. n. 2 (Cassia)]. 18 kms from the city.

Hypogeums in the neighbourhood near the parish church Pian della Colonna, Vallebona.

ISCHIA DI CASTRO (Viterbo). On the road from Valentano to Manciano (at 6,8 kms) which turns off the road that completes the way round Lake Bolsena at Valentano. (See under Bolsena).

Antiquarium in the Palazzo Comunale, and tombs in the neighbourhood.

ISOLA FARNESE - See *VEIO*.

LEPRIGNANO - See *CAPENA*.

LIVORNO [S.S. n. 1 (Aurelia)].

Museum of Archaeology and Numismatics « Enrico Chiellini », in the civic museum (Villa Fabbricotti, Piazza Matteotti).

Etruscan and pre-Etruscan antiquities from ancient *Triturrita* in the neighbourhood (Limone, Quercianella, Montenero) and from Cecina, Vada, Castagneto, Roselle, Isole d'Elba and Giannutri, etc.

LUCCA [Autostrada Firenze-Mare].

Etruscan bronzes from Ponte a Moriano, and objects from the various localities of Garfagnana (Etrusco-Ligurian) in the National Museum (Villa Guinigi, Via della Quarconia).

LUNI (La Spezia, Ortonovo). 7 kms from Sarzana [S.S. n. 1 (Aurelia)], following the Aurelia road towards Carrara as far as Piazza Granda, and then turn right.

Antiquarium of Luni.

Remains of the Etrusco-Roman theatre.

LUNI (Viterbo, Blera). See *S. GIOVENALE.*

MAGLIANO IN TOSCANA (Heba) (Grosseto). On the by-road to Ponte Albegna-Scansano, which branches off to the left of the Manciano road (10,6 kms) from Ponte Albegna on the S.S. n. 1 (Aurelia) at 175 kms.

Necropolis on the Colle Lupo, outside Porta S. Giovanni, beyond the Fosso Patrignone and the Fosso Castione.

MARSILIANA D'ALBEGNA (Caletra?) (Grosseto, Manciano).

Castle on the top of a hill on the right of the S.S. n. 74

(14 kms) which branches off the Aurelia at Ponte Albegna, and goes to Manciano. Coming from the north, turn off at 250 kms, and from the south at 146 kms.

Necropolis on the Poggio Macchiabuia to the south, and at Banditella to the N. W. (The rich contents of these tombs are housed in the Archaeological Museum in Firenze).

Many desecrated tombs in the farm n. 279.

MARZA BOTTO

MASSA MARITTIMA (Grosseto).

Turn off the S.S. n. 1 (Aurelia) at Follonica (the Siena road S.S. n. 73, 19,2 kms). From Siena 65,3 kms.

Civic Museum near the civic library (Urns, buccheri, idols, etc.).

Etruscan ruins at various sites in the neighbourhood.

MONTALCINO (Siena).

A turning 9 kms on the S.S. n. 2 (Cassia) at Torrenieri (36,7 kms to the south of Siena).

Civic Antiquarium with Etrusco-Roman objects from the vicinity and from S. Angelo in Colle.

MONTEPULCIANO (Siena).
On the S.S. n. 146 from Chiusi, or from Siena [Autostrada del Sole], or, coming from Siena towards the south on the S.S. n. 2 (Cassia), turn off at S. Quirico d'Orcia on to the S.S. n. 146 (24 kms).

Urns with inscriptions walled into the facade of the Palazzo Bucelli. Small Etruscan collection in the Palazzo Tarugi.

MONTERIGGIONI (Siena). On the S.S. n. 2 (57,4 kms from Firenze). By the superstrada, exit at Belvedere near Colle Val d'Elsa.

Tomb of the *Sepus* at *Malacena*, near the Casone on the Siena road (not far from the station of Castellina in Chianti), where, with the permission of the owners (Conti Terrosi), one can inspect the few remaining urns. The rest of this tomb is in the National Museum in East Berlin.

Not far from the Badia a Isola, on the Siena road (to the right), is a tomb which is no longer accessible, with inscriptions on the walls and a partly preserved alphabet spelling book.

MUSIGNANO (Viterbo). On the S.S. n. 312, that from Montalto di Castro turns on to the S.S. n. 1 (Aurelia).

A private collection in the Villa Torlonia.

NARCE. See *CALCATA* (in the appendix).

NEPI (Nèpete, Nepet), (Rome). On the S.S. n. 2 (Cassia), turning off at the crossroad *la Colonnetta di Nepi* (4,6 kms) at 42,8 kms.

Remains of walls and tombs.

NORCHIA (Orcle?). Ruins. (Viterbo, Vetralla).

From Vetralla, leave the S.S. n. 2 (Cassia) turning off

for Le Prata (10 kms) at Casolone, farmstead on the right of the Rio Acqua Alta, or on the S.S. n. 1 (Aurelia) turning off at 87 kms (S.S. n. 1 bis) as far as Monte Romano (14 kms).

A vast necropolis of rock-tombs with architectural facades at the pediment of the temple.

Remains of walls and gates.

Apply to the Potente restaurant for the guide. (Tour takes 3 hrs).

ORBETELLO (Subcosa?) (Grosseto). A turning off the S.S. n. 1 (Aurelia) (4 kms) at 191,7 kms (Orbetello goods yard); turn off the Aurelia at 143,1 kms.

According to some, this site was in the neighbourhood of modern *Tagliata* at the foot of the *Cosa* hill.

Remains of the encircling walls to the E., S. and W. of the city.

A museum of Etrusco-Roman antiquities in the Palazzo Pretorio (buccheri, bronzes etc.), with objects discovered in the districts of *Cosa* and *Vulci.*

ORTE (Horta) (Viterbo). [Autostrada del Sole, or on the S.S. n. 204 from Viterbo].

Civic archaeological collection of sculpture in stone and inscriptions.

Tombs with decorated pediments near the Convento dei Cappuccini to the west.

ORVIETO (Velsu, Velzna; Fanum Voltumnae?) (Terni). [Autostrada del Sole, or on the S.S. n. 71].

Museum of the Opera del Duomo in the Palazzo dei Papi (Piazza del Duomo, 26) with a sarcophagus with painted reliefs from Torre S. Severo, etc.

The *Faina* collection (Piazza del Duomo, 28). Terracottas, vases, bronzes, buccheri, etc.

An Etruscan altar in the church of S. Lorenzo in Arari.

Remains of a temple at Belvedere, near the Pozzo di S. Patrizio, or della Rocca.

Necropolis at the *Crocefisso del Tufo*, at the foot of the cliffs on which the city stands, outside the Porta Maggiore on the right.

Three painted tombs, one near the Castel Rubello, and the other two on the mount called « Poggio dei Sette Camini » (or *del Roccolo*), to the S. W. of the city. These can be reached by the by-road to Porano (turning off to the left from the Cassia road for Rome at Ponte del Marchese).

PALESTRINA (PRAENESTE)

PERUGIA (Perusia). [Autostrada del Sole, Bettole tollgate].

Remains of walls. Arch of Augustus and Porta Marzia. National Archaeological Museum of Umbria (prehistoric and Etrusco-Roman) in the ex-convent of S. Dominico (Piazza G. Bruno, 10). Inscriptions, urns, etc.

In the civic library are books and miscellaneous writings on Etruscology by the noted archaeologist Ariodante Fabretti (1816-94).

Hypogeum (a reconstruction with the original doorway) at Villa Sperandio (owner Judge Ernesto Sallusti) with contents.

Ipogeo dei Volumni at the Palazzone near the level crossing just before Ponte S. Giovanni (1 km. from the station of the same name), with the small museum of the Palazzone.

Tomba di S. Manno, with a long inscription (belonging to the Knights of Malta), near the S.S. n. 75 bis (about 5 kms, short by-road to the right of the village of S. Manno.

PIENZA (Siena). On the S.S. n. 146, turning off at S. Quirico d'Orcia from the S.S. n. 2 (Cassia).

Urns and inscriptions beneath the loggia and in the garden of the Palazzo Piccolomini. Small Etruscan museum annexed to the cathedral (Via del Casello, 1).

PISA. On the S.S. n. 1 (Aurelia). [S.S. n. 67, and Autostrada Firenze-Mare, Lucca toll-gate].

Museum of the Opera della Primaziale: a few Etrusco-Roman antiquities under the porticos of the Camposanto.

PITIGLIANO (Grosseto). On the S.S. n. 74, 62,5 kms from Orbetello (S.S. n. 1 (Aurelia); or 27 kms from S. Lorenzo Nuovo [S.S. n. 2 (Cassia)], at the north end of Lake Bolsena.

Civic museum in the Palazzo Ponti in the Piazza del Duomo, with Etruscan antiquities discovered in the districts: Pitigliano, Sovana, Poggio Buco, Naioli, Terralba, Formica.

Remains of Etrusco-Roman walls at Pietra Lata (Capo di Sotto).

POGGIO BUCO (Statonia?) (Grosseto, Pitigliano). 1 km S. W. to the left of the Ponte sul Fiora, on the S.S. n. 74.

Necropolis and remains of the city.

POPULONIA (Fufluna, Pupluna) (Livorno, Piombino). Turn off the S.S. n. 1 (Aurelia) at S. Vincenzo (Coming from the north), or at Venturina (Coming from the south), or from Piombino (Strada della Principessa).

To the S. W. of the present day city, walls of the ancient acropolis. The circuit goes from Golfo di Baratti to the « Cala S. Quirico », across the Poggio Guardiola. At the bottom near the Porto Baratti (S. Cerbone, Poggio della Porcareccia, Poggio delle Granate, Le Grotte, Le Buche delle Fate), a vast necropolis with tombs of various periods.

Etruscan museum of local antiquities in the Villa della Società Populonia Italica at the top of the hill.

PORTO S. STEFANO (Grosseto, Monte Argentario). Turn off the S.S. n. 1 (Aurelia) at Orbetello.

Etrusco-Roman antiquities in the Pensione Miramare (owner Stirabelli).

QUINTO (Firenze, Sesto Fiorentino). To the N. W. of Firenze near Sesto on the S.S. n. 64.

Tomb under the Villa Pecchioli-Gerbi at La Mula (Via Gramsci, 269), or from the Via della Mula, 2 (turning to the right).

Another ancient tomb is *La Montagnola* in the Villa Cantagalli, in Via Fratelli Rosselli, 17 (to the right of the castle after the ex-Villa Reale).

Other remains in the vicinity.

RADICOFANI (Siena). On the S.S. n. 2 (Cassia), 67 kms to the south of Siena.

Ancient objects in private houses.

Remains of polygonal walls.

ROSELLE (Rusellae). Ruins. (Grosseto). On a hill 1 km to the right of Via Rosellana (turn off before the Ponte sul Rio Salica, at about 7,8 kms from Grosseto by the road which leads to Paganico and Monte Amiata, after which the road becomes a rough lane.

Remains of walls and gates, various buildings and the necropolis.

ROSIGNANO MARITTIMO (Livorno). Turn off the S.S. n. 1 (Aurelia) at Rosignano Solvay (4,2 kms), 43,4 kms from Pisa.

Civic antiquarium.

Castle of Rosignano Alto (Apply to the custodian of

the Comune); Etrusco-Roman antiquities in the vicinity of Castiglioncello.

SAN GIMIGNANO (Siena). From Poggibonsi on the S.S. n. 2 (Cassia) it is 11,1 kms, or from Colle Val d'Elsa on the S.S. n. 68 it is 12,9 kms.

Small collection of Etruscan antiquities in a room of the Civic Museum, and in the large cloister of the Chiesa di S. Agostino from the neighbouring excavations (Poggio ad Assi, Bucciano, Sferracavalli); at Cellole, at La Ripa and at Pistaccio, late Etruscan tombs. Objects in the care of the curator.

SAN GIOVENALE (Viterbo, Blera). Between Blera and Civitella Cesi. Turn off the S.S. n. 1 bis at Monte Romano, which is reached by turning off the S.S. n. 1 (Aurelia) at 87 kms near the Mignone stream (locality of Luni).

Remains of an Etruscan city in the acropolis, a necropolis, near the ruins of a mediaeval castle.

SAN GIULIANO. See *BARBARANO ROMANO*.

SANTA MARINELLA. See *SANTA SEVERA*.

SANTA SEVERA (Pyrgi) (Rome, Santa Marinella). On the S.S. n. 1 (Aurelia) to the south of Civitavecchia. Remains of the ancient port of *Caere*. Remains of walls beneath the castle, a conduit near the dockyard, and an Etrusco-Punic shrine from whence originate amongst other things, three small inscribed gold laminae, two in Etruscan and one in Punic, with the dedication to *Uni-Astarte,* very important for the understanding of the Etruscan civilization. These are now in the Villa Giulia, Rome.

SASSI CADUTI

SATURNIA (Grosseto, Manciano). 13 kms from Manciano (S.S. n. 74) on the summit of a travertine height, from which stretches the road between Manciano (13,5 kms) and Arcidosso.

Remains of walls outside Porta Romana. Necropolis especially at Puntone nel Piano di Palma (about 40 minutes from the mule track to the north).

SIENA (Sena, Saena). [S.S. n. 2 (Cassia)].

Archaeological Museum at no. 1, Via della Sapienza, together with the collection from the *Accademia dei Fisio-critici,* and other objects (buccheri, urns, bronzes, sculpture) from the territory of Siena.

SOVANA (Suana) (Grosseto, Sorano). 9 kms from Piti-gliano (turn off the S.S. n. 74 at S. Lucia below Pitigliano), a little more than 3 kms from the short cut (a mule track) that joins up past the Ponte S. Rocco over the Lente (N. E.).

Interesting necropolis (guide needed), with rock-tombs with architectural facades (at Poggio Stanziale, tombs of the *Grotta di Pola, La Colonnata,* the *Tifone,* etc.; at Sopraripa, the tombs *della Sirena* or *del Pischero*). Burial

chambers without architectural facades (Cava di S. Seba-
stiano, Campo della Zinza, Campo della Cura, etc.).

SUTRI (Sutrium) (Viterbo). On the S.E., n. 2 (Cassia) to
the south of Viterbo.

Etruscan necropolis to the S.E., below the little church
of the Madonna del Parto; immediately beneath the city is
the Etrusco-Roman amphitheatre excavated in the tufo rock.
To visit this apply to the sacristan in the Duomo. Other
tombs in the neighbourhood. Remains of gates. Antiquarium
in the Palazzo Comunale.

TALAMONE

TARQUINIA [formerly *Corneto Tarquinia*]. *(Tarquinii)*.
(Rome). Turn off (2,5 kms) at 101 kms on the S.S. n. 1
(Aurelia) near the station of the same name.

National Museum of Tarquinian antiquities in the Palazzo Vitelleschi, Piazza Cavour, 1 (in which are incorporated
the Civic Museum and the Bruschi-Falgari collection):
sarcophagi, etc.

A vast necropolis on the hill *I Monterozzi* (apply to
the custodian of the tombs at the museum), and in the
environs, to the S.E. of the city along the road to Vetralla,
many accessible painted tombs of the greatest interest and
unique of their kind, each one distinguished by its name and
number.

Remains of walls and part of the ancient city on the
hill beyond the Fosso S. Savino.

TOMB OF BULLS, AUGURS, LEOPARDS

TOSCANELLA. See *TUSCANIA*.   *BARONS, TYPHONS,*

ORCO, & FISH.

TREVIGNANO (Viterbo, Acquapendente). Turn off the S.S. n. 2 (Cassia) on to a track at Centeno (between Acquapendente and Radicofani).

Small Bourbon del Monte collection.

TUSCANIA [formerly *Toscanella*] (Viterbo). About halfway between Viterbo (23 kms) and Tarquinia (27 kms). Turn off the S.S. n. 2 (Cassia) at 70 kms and follow the road which joins up with the S.S. n. 1 (Aurelia), or at 101 kms, turn off the Aurelia, passing through Tarquinia.

Tomb *Grotta della Regina* beneath the church of the Madonna dell'Olivo, 1,5 kms on the by-road outside the Porta del Poggio, with galleries at several levels, and a little further on, the *Tomba del Carcarello* (in the farm of the same name). Many sarcophagi lids in terracotta in the *Tomba della Televisione* (which restarted the excavation) in the area of Pian di Mola.

VEIANO (Viterbo). Turn off the S.S. n. 2 (Cassia) to Manziana on the Via Claudia.

Grottoes (tombs) to the S. W. of the hill.

VEIO (Veii). Ruins. Near Isola Farnese (Rome). On the S.S. n. 2 (Cassia) 17 kms to the north of Rome.

Apply to the custodian of the antiquities in the area of the temple.

Remains of galleries and conduits. *Ponte Sodo* over the Fosso del Crémera. *Campana* tomb to the N. E., with archaic paintings. (A part of the contents is in the Gregorian Etruscan Museum in the Vatican, and the other part in the National Museum of Villa Giulia).

Necropolis on Monte S. Michele.

Remains of the acropolis in the Cittadella or Piazza d'Armi, to the S. E.

Tomba delle Anatre with painted lines (7th century B.C.) in the « Riserva del Bagno ».

Remains of the foundations of the Etruscan temple and a sacrificial altar at Portonaccio.

VETULONIA [formerly *Colonna*] *(Vetalu, Vetluna)* (Grosseto, Castiglion della Pescaia). 10 kms from the S.S. n. 1 (Aurelia) turning off near Giuncarico.

Remains of walls of Arx and city. Beneath the city to the N. E., a vast necropolis (guide needed), with numerous tombs of various epochs. Several isolated tombs, especially the Tombs *della Pietrera* and *del Diavolino,* that are situated along a track that turns to the right from the road that goes down to « I Grilli ». A small antiquarium.

VIGNANELLO (Viterbo). On the road that turns off the S.S. n. 3 (Flaminia) near Civita Castellana, or 17,3 kms from Viterbo.

Tombs with inscriptions and architectural ornaments, especially at La Cupa and Poggio Castello.

VITERBO (Surina?, Vicus Elbii). [S.S. n. 2 (Cassia)].

Civic Museum in the church of S. Maria della Verità,

outside the gate of the same name (sarcophagi, inscriptions, etc.).

The Ponte del Castello, formerly called *d'Ercole* and now *di S. Lorenzo*, is Etruscan.

The bridge over the Bulicame, called *Ponte Camillano* is Roman; it is to the west outside Porta Fiorentina, near the road to the Baths.

VOLTERRA (Velathri, Volaterrae) (Pisa). On the S.S. n. 68 from Cecina to Colle Val d'Elsa.

Remains of a Roman theatre in Vallebuona. (Guardiola), Porta dell'Arco and Porta Diana or Portone.

Tombs especially two at « I Marmini », outside Porta Diana, (always accessible).

Guarnacci Museum (Palazzo Desideri-Tangassi, Via Don Minzoni, 15): prehistoric section, in prevalence with remains of the Villanovian civilization; Etruscan section, with stelae, urns especially in alabaster, aes-grave, votive statuettes in terracotta and bronze, mirrors, gold necklaces, glass, etc.; Roman section, with epigraphs and objects from the Roman theatre.

Remains of a Roman theatre in Vallebuona.

VULCI (Vulcia, Volci). Ruins. (Viterbo, Montalto di Castro). Turn off the S.S. n. 1 (Aurelia) at 109 kms on to the road for Valentano.

Turning to the left at 13,4 kms, one arrives at Castello Torlonia, where there is an antiquarium containing selected

pieces, near the picturesque Etrusco-Roman Ponte dell'Abbidia, on the Musignano estate. Remains of Etruscan buildings near which are some tombs.

Necropolis on the left bank of the Fiora (Comune of Canino to the north of Ponte Sodo over Fosso Timone (can be reached directly by the road that branches off to the left of the road for Valentano (5 kms) from Montalto), with tumuli tombs (cuccumella and cuccumelletta), and burial chambers, some with magnificent pictures, now kept in the Torlonia private museum, Rome; the tomb *François* (taking the road that goes to the left at 6 kms), and that *delle Iscrizioni* (a guide is obligatory. Apply to the Castello Torlonia).

Beyond the Abbazia, remains of the city.

APPENDIX

Places that have supplied etrusco-roman material, but whose antiquities are no longer accessible or only with difficulty

ANTELLA (Firenze, Bagno a Ripoli).

Spurious rock inscriptions in the vicinity, on the Poggio di Firenze, at the « Palazzaccio Diruto ».

CALCATA (Narce) (Viterbo).

Traces of walls and drains.

Necropolis at the foot of the hill.

CAMPAGNANO DI ROMA (Rome).

Ruins of tombs containing archaic vases in the Villa Giulia museum, Rome.

CAPRÀNICA (Viterbo).

Tombs (grottoes) in the neighbourhood.

CARBOGNANO (Viterbo).

Tombs in the neighbourhood.

CASTEL CARDINALE (Musarna) (Viterbo).

Tombs at « Macchia del Conte », etc.

CIVITELLA S. PAOLO (Rome).

Remains of tombs the contents of which are in the Villa Giulia museum, Rome.

CIVITÙCOLA. See *CAPENA.*

ELBA (ISLAND OF) (Livorno).

Prehistoric and Etrusco-Roman material was found on Monte Giove near Marciana, at Cima del Monte, Lacona, Laconella, Valle d'Inferno, Ponza.

Objects in the Villa Romana from the *Grotte* (antiquarium) the remains of which were found 5 kms from Portoferraio.

MANCIANO (Grosseto).

Tombs in the vicinity. Traces of the ancient city on Colle Sparne.

MONTERANO (Manturanum) (Rome, Canale Monterano).

Etruscan necropolis.

MORLUPO (Rome). 2 kms.

Remains of tombs, the contents of which are in the Villa Giulia, Rome.

Remains of the old port of Tarquinia to the north.

PORTO CLEMENTINO (Graviscae) (Rome, Tarquinia).
Remains of the ancient harbour of Tarquinia at the N.

RIANO (Rome).
Remains of tombs, the contents of which are in the Villa Giulia, Rome.

SARTEANO (Siena).
Etruscan tombs at Solaia.

VAIANO (Perugia, Castiglion del Lago).
Tombs at Bruscalupo.

IMPORTANT MUSEUMS CONTAINING ETRUSCAN COLLECTIONS IN OTHER PARTS OF ITALY

TRENTINO

TRENTO - National Museum (Castello del Buon Consiglio, Via B. Clesio, 5).
Situla with inscription, from Cembra, etc.

PIEDMONT

NOVARA - Civic Museum of the Broletto (Palazzo del Mercato).
Etruscan antiquities.

TURIN - Museum of antiquities (Palazzo dell'Accademia delle Scienze, Via Accademia delle Scienze, 6).

Etruscan vases, urns, etc.

LIGURIA

CHIAVARI - Small museum of the Istituto di Studi Liguri in Via Vittorio Veneto, 23.

Archaic Liguri-Etruscan necropolis (excavation in progress).

GENOA - Civic Museum of Ligurian archaeology (Villa Durazzo-Pallavicini (Genova-Pegli).

Stelae statues from Lunigiana, etc.

LA SPEZIA - Civic Museum (Corso Cavour, 39).

Stelae statues from the Val di Magra. Paletnological collection. Lunese Archaeological Museum, with objects from the former Fabbricotti private museum at Carrara.

LOMBARDY

BRESCIA - Archaeological Museum (Via dei Musei, 57).

Etruscan vases. Neolithic and Eneolithic antiquities from Arezzo and Orvieto.

LODI (Milan) - Civic Museum (Corso Umberto I, 63).

Objects of the Etruscan epoch from different excavations.

MANTOVA - Gallery and museum in the Palazzo Ducale (Piazza Sordello).

Prehistoric objects and Etruscan antiquities.

MILAN - Museum of Ancient Art (in the Castello Sforzesco).

Prehistoric and Etruscan antiquities: Golasecca collection (in the Archaeological Museum in the Monastero Maggiore, Corso Magenta, 15).

Numismatic collection of the Archaeological Museum [formerly in the Palazzo del Museo (Brera)]. Series of Etruscan coins.

PAVIA - Antiquarium of the Istituto di Archaeology dell'Università.

Etruscan bronzes and prehistoric objects partly from the territory of Etruria Padana.

VENETIA

ADRIA (Rovigo) - Archaeological Museum (Piazzale Etruschi, 2).

A few objects of local Etruscan civilization; Aretine and Etrusco-Campani vases.

VERONA - Maffei Lapidarian Museum (Philharmonic Theatre, Piazza Bra).

Cinerary urns with Etruscan inscriptions and decorations in relief.

Archaeological Museum in the Roman Theatre: urns, vases, bronzes.

EMILIA

BOLOGNA - Civic Museum (Via Archiginnasio, 2, Portico del Pavaglione).

Archaeological section with rich prehistoric and classical collection from the pre-Etruscan and Etruscan necropolis of Felsina.

Bronze situla, stelae with bas-reliefs, and other objects from Certosa.

Terracottas from Civita Alba and antiquities from Etruria proper.

Gozzadini Museum (Civic library of Archiginnasio, Piazza Galvani, 1, Portico del Pavaglione).

Objects from Villanova.

FERRARA - National Archaeological Museum (Palazzo di Ludovico il Moro, Via XX Settembre, 124).

Objects from the Greek-Etruscan necropolis of Spina.

FORLÌ - Archaeological Museum (Corso della Repubblica, 32).

Objects from Villanova.

MARZABOTTO (Bologna), on the Via Porrettana. Small Etruscan 'Pompeo Aria' museum containing local antiquities.

Necropolis and remains of temples in the park of the villa.

Outlines and remains of a city *(Misa)* at Piana di Misano.

MODENA - Civic Museum (Palazzo dei Musei, Largo Porta S. Agostino, 48).

Paletnological collection with material of the *Terremare.*

PARMA - National Museum of Antiquities (Palazzo della Pilotta, Piazza Marconi).

Antiquities of the *Terremare.*

PIACENZA - Civic Museum (Palazzo Gazzola, Via San Tommaso, 14).

Inscribed haruspical bronze liver from Settima.

REGGIO NELL'EMILIA - Chierici Paletnological Museum (Civic Museum, Via Lazzaro Spallanzani, 1).

Rich material of the *Terremare* epoch (utensils, bone objects, spindles, pottery, and metal arms).

MARCHE

ANCONA - National Museum of the « Marche », Palazzo Ferretti, (Piazza S. Francesco).

Very rich examples of objects from the Paleolithic, Neolithic, Bronze and Iron ages (including typical specimens from Novilara and Pianello).

PESARO - Archaeological Museum (Via Mazza, 97).
Bilingual inscriptions on the stelae from Novilara, etc.

RIMINI (Forlì) - Civic Museum (Via Gambalunga, 5).
Objects from Villanova and from the tombs at Verrucchio.

UMBRIA [1]

ASSISI (Perugia) - Civic Museum (Via Portica, 2).
Graeco-Etruscan cippus and Etruscan cinerary urn.

BETTONA (Vettona) (Perugia) - Civic Museum (Palazzo
del Podestà, Piazza Cavour).
Inscriptions and sculpture. At Colle an Etruscan
hypogeum.

FOLIGNO (Perugia) - Archaeological Museum (Palazzo
Trinci, Piazza della Repubblica).
Etruscan inscriptions.

TODI (Perugia) - Civic Museum (Palazzo del Comune).
Various Etruscan and Umbrian-Etruscan antiquities
(gold and silver objects, bronzes and terracottas). Rich
collection of Etruscan coins from Todi.

---

[1] See also part I.

LATIUM [1]

CITTÀ DEL VATICANO. (See *ROME*).

GROTTAFERRATA (Rome) - Badia Museum.
  Inscriptions and Etruscan vases.

LANUVIO (formerly *Civitia Lavinia*) (Rome).
  Civic collection (Palazzo del Comune).
  Italo-Etruscan objects (VI-III century B. C.) from the temple of *Iuno Sospita*; antefixae, tiles and entablatures.

PALESTRINA (Rome) - National Archaeological Museum in the Palazzo Barberini.
  Archaeological material from Latium.

ROME - Capitolino dei Conservatori Museum.
  Bronze wolf: Italo-Etruscan antiquities and objects from Caere in the « Sala dei Fasti ».
  Barracco Museum (168, Corso Vittorio Emanuele).
  Funerary bas-reliefs from Chiusi.
  Gregorian Etruscan Museum in the Vatican City.
  Material from southern Etruria and especially from the *Regolini - Galassi* tomb at Cervéteri; statue of « Mars » from Todi: sarcophagus of Adonis from Tuscania, etc.

---

  [1] See also part I.

National Museum of Latian Antiquities in the Villa
Giulia (Palazzo di Papa Giulio, Via delle Belle Arti).
Faliscan, Villanovian and Latian antiquities, decorative
terracottas, material from the Barberini tombs at Palestrina,
Ficoroni cista, the Apollo of Veio, etc.

National Roman Museum (Baths of Diocletian).

Coins, medals, etc. from the Kirchner Museum.

Villa Albani Museum (Via Salaria). Material and pictures
from Vulci.

National Gallery of Ancient Art (formerly the Corsini
Gallery) (Lungara, 10).

The Corsini Chair.

The Luigi Pigorini Prehistorical-Ethnographical Museum.
(Palazzo delle Scienze, at the E.U.R.).

Material from the Bernardini tomb at Palestrina.

CAMPANIA

CAPUA (Naples) - Provincial Museum of Campania (Via
Roma, 68).

Terracottas from the sanctuary Le Curti.

PADULA (Salerno) - Archaeological Museum of Western
Lucania at Certosa di S. Lorenzo, with material from Padula
and Sala Consilina *(Consilinum, Tanagra?)*.

SANTA MARIA CAPUA VETERE (Caserta) - Antiquarium
(Piazza 1° Ottobre 1860).

Sculptural, epigraphic and architectural material from the ruins of Capua and Casilinum.

SALERNO - Provincial Museum at S. Benedetto.
Villanovian antiquities from Pontecagnano and other localities.

SICILY

PALERMO - National Archaeological Museum (Piazza Olivella).
Etruscan antiquities from Chiusi, from the Casuccini collection.

A SHORT SUMMARY OF THE HISTORY,
CIVILISATION, LANGUAGE AND ART
OF THE ETRUSCANS

CHIUSI, Museum.
Female figure on a cinerary urn.

I

HISTORY AND CIVILISATION

Origin of the Etruscans.

« The Lydians themselves say that the games now in use among themselves and among the Greeks, were of their own invention. They assert that at the time these games were invented, they also colonized Thyrenia and in connection with this event they relate as follows:

« During the reign of Atys, son of Manes, a terrible famine prevailed in all Lydia. For some time the people supported it with patience but when they saw the evil still continuing, they sought for remedies and some devised one thing and some another...

« As the famine did not abate but, on the contrary, became still more acute, the King divided the Lydians into two parts and cast lots which should remain and which quit the country and he appointed himself King over those whose lot it should be to stay, while over those who were to emigrate, he appointed as King his own son whose name was Tyrrhenus.

« Those to whose lot it fell to leave their country went down to Smyrna, built ships, and having put all things necessary on board, they set sail in search of food and land till having passed by many nations, they reached the Umbrians where they founded cities and dwell to this day. And from being called Lydians, they changed their name to that of the King's son who had led them and called themselves Tyrrhenians ».

This story which we read in the Histories of Herodotus (Vol. I, Chap. 94) is our only original, reliable, literary source of information as to the origin of the Etruscans, who are the *Tyrseni* or *Tyrrheni* of the Grek text, and the transformation of the name is due, according to some, to transposition of the *r* and the amplification of the syllable *turs.* The whole account is however so fantastic and unreal, as to make many scholars believe that Herodotus was only quoting a legendary tradition.

Those who follow the historian Dionysius of Halicarnassus, believe that the Etruscans were an indigenous race calling themselves *Rasena*: others again are of opinion that they descended into Italy from the Rhaetian Alps between the XIII and XI centuries B.C. Today three principal theories prevail:

1) The Etruscans descended from the Alps into the valley of the Po, driving out before them inhabitants of the *terramare* or prehistoric dwellings on lakes or marshy land during the bronze age.

2) The Etruscans were already settled in central Italy during the first iron age and their civilisation may have arisen from the fusion of two great ethnical strata: the *Italo-lacustrian* tribes (whose funeral rite was inhumation)

already existing in Italy in the neolithic age and the *terra-mare* tribes who disposed of their dead by cremation and who came down into Italy from the north in the bronze age. There would also have been infiltrations of oriental influence, due, probably, to commercial intercourse.

3) The Etruscans are to be identified with the Villa-novians and were the actual descendants of the Lake-dwellers and *terramare* tribes (no ethnical distinction exists between the two) who were present in the peninsula during the early neolithic age.

On the other hand archaeological researches seem to confirm — though not without certain contradictions — the Asiatic or Aegean origin of the Etruscans who brought the breath of a new civilisation among the Umbrians of central Italy. It was a complex, oriental civilisation owing to the different peoples with whom it had been in contact, and it was destined to have a powerful influence on the civilisation of the iron age in Italy and on Umbrian art which was in a state of stagnation and might otherwise have employed centuries on its development, or might have developed on quite different lines owing to more direct contact with Greek colonists who would certainly have pushed their way through Italy from south to north, uncontested conquerors.

But even admitting that the Etruscans entered Italy by way of the sea, it is not likely that their immigration took place all at once. At first there were probably small expeditions which came into contact with the Umbrians towards the end of the IX and the beginning of the VIII century B. C., until in the last decades of the latter century, the Etruscans first established themselves stably on the sea-

coast which still bears their name, the Tyrrhenian Sea. On
the strength of the story of Hellanicus Lesbius, quoted by
Dionysius who refutes it, there are those who insist that
the Etruscans, though coming from the shores of Greece
or Asia Minor, first landed in Italy on the Adriatic coast,
at Spina, near the mouth of the Po, whence they penetrated
into the interior of the peninsula, in a south-westerly
direction.

DEVELOPMENT AND EXPANSION.

The Etruscan occupation of central Italy came about
gradually between the VIII and the VI century B. C.; it
spread both in the interior and along the coast, towards the
north, finally covering a vast region which, at the moment
of its greatest development, was bounded on the north by
the river Magra, north-east and east by the Apennines, east
and south by the Tiber. This constituted Etruria proper,
where Etruscan civilisation reached its greatest splendour
and revealed itself in the fullness and multiplicity of its
various aspects [1], but the total extent of territory occupied
by the Etruscan people was at one time far larger than
that comprised within these limits. Traces of their art have
been found north of the Apennines, in the Bolognese district
and in the region beyond it, known as Etruria Circumpadana,
where they founded a number of cities including, besides

---

[1] In the Ist century of our era, under the Emperor Augustus,
this part of the peninsula formed the VIIth region of Italy.

one (Misa?) of which some remains still exist near Marzabotto, Felsina, Modena, Parma, Melpo, Mantova, Spina, and Adria. To the south, where Latium was already under their rule (see Chapter III) the Etruscans pushed forward into the plain of Campania, founded Capua (Volturno) and Nola, perhaps also Pompeii and entered Picenum. By the beginning of the VI century B.C., Etruscan civilisation, starting from central Italy, had attracted into its own orbit and assimilated the populations of Umbria, Latium, Emilia, part of Campania, Liguria and Lombardy; it possibly reached even to Corsica, the possession of which was being contested by the Phocaeans and the Carthaginians. From Lombardy in the north to the river Sele in the south and even further, the Etruscan people carried on their work of civilisation and regeneration: having once accomplished it, they disappeared, leaving a rich heritage of art and culture to be taken up by other hands and given back under another name, to the whole world. Etrurian culture penetrated into Rome from its earliest days, indeed, there seems some reason to believe that the Eternal City may actually have been founded by the Etruscans.

The eventual decline of the Etruscan nation was brought about partly by natural causes such epidemics of malaria in the central and southern parts, partly by military defeats. These factors united to produce the gradual collapse of Etruscan power in the III-I centuries B.C.

The Confederation of Etruria proper consisted of twelve States or Cities and was therefore called *dodecapolis*. One of the most ancient cities was *Tarquinii,* the Etruscan Metropolis, to which were added, in process of time, *Vulci,*

4.

Vetulonia, Caere (now Cervéteri) *Arezzo, Chiusi (Chamars), Roselle, Volterra (Velathri), Cortona, Perugia, Volsinii (Velzu), Veii,* afterwards substituted by *Populonia,* perhaps also *Fiesole.* Other notable cities were *Pisa, Sovana, Saturnia, Statonia, Talamone, Cosa, Tuscania* and lastly *Luni.* On the height of Montefiascone (?) or of Orvieto stood the celebrated *fanum Voltumnae* where solemn religious ceremonies took place every spring, attended by immense crowds of people from all parts of Etruria.

Each of the twelve cities of Etruria was ruled by a *lucumo* or king, chosen from among the eldest sons of the noble or princely families, descendants of the original colonists. These Lucumones also exercised judicial powers and it is interesting to note, in this connection, that the Roman symbol of justice, the *lictor's fasces*, is of purely Etruscan origin, as also the fact that the lictors were twelve in number.

The priestly authority and all the sacred mysteries of the « Etruscan discipline » were in the hands of the king. After the military and sacerdotal aristocracy came the *plebs*, consisting of the masses of conquered Umbrians who cultivated the soil and formed the nucleus of the army in time of war. A burgher or citizen class was evolved gradually in course of time, during the transformation of the monarchical system of government into a republican régime, which took place in the VI and V centuries B.C. There are also isolated instances of social revolutions carried even to excess (see the following pp.).

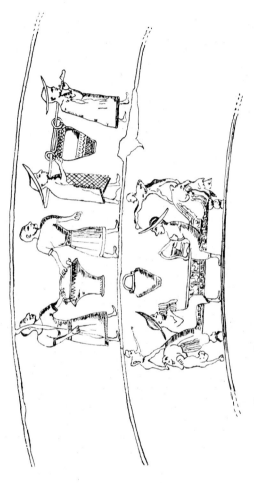

BOLOGNA. Civic Museum. *Detail of family life engraved around a bronze situla from Felsina.*

The citizens were divided into three tribes, according to their degree of social position as descendants of the original colonists and the army was also divided into three categories of soldiers.

POLITICAL POWER AND HISTORICAL VICISSITUDES.

It is well known that an Etruscan dynasty reigned in Rome from 623 to 510 B.C., the three last kings being Tarquinius Priscus, Servius Tullius and Tarquinius Superbus, and that Rome continued to be subject to the Etruscans under Lars Porsena, king of Clusium, who was called to his aid by the last Tarquinius when his subjects expelled him from his throne. Their rule was even more powerful and durable in the district north of Rome, among the *Falisci* who became incorporated with the Etruscans.

By the end of the VI century B.C. the territory covered by the Etruscan nation had reached its greatest extension, while its land and sea power had increased so much that it was able to compete with Greece and Carthage for predominance in Italy, but the political hegemony of Etruria was of brief duration for in the early years of the following century Rome freed herself by land and Cumae by sea, giving a check to Etruscan expansion and marking the beginning of its decay.

After the Roman victory over the Latin League at Lake Regillus, about 496 B.C., the formation of a Latin State with Rome at its head brought about the rise of a new power on the southern borders of Etruria proper. The two Confederations soon came into conflict with one another and the Etruscans found themselves cut off from land communication with their colonies in Campania. There was a long and fierce struggle between Rome and the opulent and powerful city of Veii, a struggle caused by the conduct of the Latin city of Fidenae which threw off the yoke of Rome and declared for Veii. The first war lasted from about 485 to 475 and ended with a Roman victory and a suspension of arms which lasted until 438. The second war ended in 425 with a fresh truce but fighting broke out again in 406 and was only brought to a conclusion in 396 with the fall of Veii, now exhausted by strife and abandoned to its fate by the other cities of the Etruscan League. This victory opened the way into Etruria for the Romans who pushed on towards the north and soon occupied Capena, Nepete and Sutrium.

The year in which peace was concluded after the first war between Rome and Veii, saw the Etruscans involved in a disastrous struggle for the possession of Cumae which, in the hands of the Greeks, formed an obstacle to their maritime communications with Capua. A century earlier when the Phocaeans threatened Corsica, the Carthaginians had helped the Etruscans to drive them out, but the Carthaginians were now engaged in defending themselves against the Romans and the Etruscans suffered a terrible naval defeat off Cumae, at the hands of the united Cumaean and Syracusan fleets commanded by Hieron. Not long afterwards, in the second half of the V century, Cumae was conquered by the Samnites and Etruria lost all her sway in Campania.

But the greatest danger to the Etruscan Confederation was to come from the north. At the beginning of the IV century B. C., hordes of Gauls crossed the Alps and invaded Etruria Circumpadana, conquering the region little by little until by the middle of the century it had become *Gallia Cisalpina*. Bands of Gauls, as is well known, pushed on to Clusium and from there to Rome. It was at this time that some groups of Etruscan refugees fled to the valleys of the Alps, and settled in Venetia Tridentina, where they gave origin to the Rhaetians, whose language and toponomy are much akin to those of the Etruscans. Those who believe that the Etruscans originally descended into Italy by land from the north, find their theory confirmed by this similitude and complete it by placing the Etruscan occupation of the Rhaetian Alps some centuries earlier.

In the meantime the powerful Syracusan navy sailed up the Tyrrhenian sea, sacking and destroying the flourishing Etruscan cities along the coast. Southern Etruria made a last effort to shake off the Roman yoke. After several isolated and unsuccessful attempts on the part of the Tarquinians and the Falisci (383-2 B.C.) Caere came to their assistance but with disastrous results, for in 351 the proud Etruscan city was obliged to submit to Rome, without however being forced to undergo the fate of Veii. Caere was detached from the League of the Twelve Cities and given a special autonomy of her own which was more apparent then real, the inhabitants becoming Roman citizens but without political rights, or privileges. At the same time a truce of forty years was stipulated with Tarquinia.

From this period the formidable power of Rome was ever on the increase and Etruria awoke — too late — to a sense of the doom impending on the whole nation. She reestablished the League on a more strictly political basis and besieged Sutrium (311-10 B. C.). Rome rushed at once to the rescue with two legions which crossed the Ciminian Hills and invaded central and eastern Etruria, meeting and defeating the Etruscan toops in a battle near Perugia. This was followed by a thirty years' peace, concluded with some of the Etruscan cities, and later by a truce established with the whole nation and renewable year by year. Tarquinia had a harder fate. She was obliged to cede part of her territory and stipulate a separate peace of forty years, in 308, B. C.

But a few years later, in 299, the Etruscans again took the offensive, allying themselves this time with their ex-enemies, the Gauls, who were also threatened by the Romans with a loss of the sites they had recently occupied in central Italy. A first expedition against the Roman regions north of the Tiber was followed up by an important alliance with the Samnites, the Umbrians and the Sabines. This brings us to the Third Samnite War (299-90). So far as the Etruscans are concerned, they were first defeated at Volterra in 298 and afterwards at Sentinum (Umbria) in a terrible battle that cost the life of the Consul, Publius Decius, while 10.000 of the Allies are said to have perished. This figure is undoubtedly exaggerated but it is significant as showing the extent of the disaster. Then followed an alliance on mild conditions between Rome and some of the principal cities of central Etruria.

Nine years later, the Senonian Gauls crossed the Apennines and asked help from Arezzo but the city remained faithful to Rome and two legions were promptly sent in its defence, commanded by the Consul, L. Cecilius Metellus, who was killed in the signal defeat suffered here by the Romans. After other vicissitudes, a new alliance was formed between the Etruscans and the Gauls (Senones and Boii) who met the Roman legions commanded by the Consul P. Cornelius Dolabella at the Vadimonian Lake (now Lago di Bassano) and this time it was the turn of the Allies to be completely routed.

Among the first consequences of this unfortunate war must be reckoned the rapid decline of Vulci which was deprived of the greater part of its territory for the benefit of Roman colonists. In 272 *Caere* too was forced to yield up half its territory and 265 saw the end of *Volsinii* the inhabitants of which were forced by the victorious Romans — after a siege in aid of the families of the place who had been exiled by their slaves — to transfer their city to another in the plain, *Volsinii [Novi]*, lacking the commanding position that had made the Volsiniens powerful and had enabled them to offer such strenuous resistance to the Roman yoke.

Etruria was now open to the Romans, especially after the destruction, in 241, of *Falerii Veteres,* the capital of the Faliscians, which constituted the last Etruscan bulwark towards the south, and it became the scene of many a fierce fight between the Roman legions and the Cisalpine and

Transalpine Gauls. The Etruscans furnished a contingent in aid of the latter but at the battle of Telamon (225 B. C.) the Romans won a signal victory that cost them, however, the life of one of their Consuls, C. Attilius Regulus, who had left Sardinia to join his fellow Consul, Emilius Papus.

The second Punic War, when Hannibal crossed the Alps and entered Italy, was fraught with disastrous consequences for the Etruscans but they remained faithful to Rome and furnished her with contingents of soldiers and supplies of provisions. In recognition of their loyalty which lasted during the War of the Allies (91 B. C.), the Lex Julia giving the right of Roman citizenship was extended to the Etruscan territory.

The Etruscan cities received a final blow from the vengance of Sylla who punished them savagely for having dared to range themselves in favour of Marius. Among those that suffered were Florence, Faesule, Volterra and Arezzo, where the Romans placed permanent military colonies as a rapid means of bringing about the extinction of the Etruscan nation. Nor were these the only cities to feel the ire of Rome; witness the destruction of Perugia by Octavius Caesar (40, B. C.) because the citizens had given refuge to Lucius Antonius, the brother of the triumvir.

From this moment the Etruscan nation ceases to have a history. Its territory was merged into the VII region of Italy when the country was partitioned by Emperor Augustus and was afterwards united to Umbria in the time of Diocletian, under the denomination of *Tuscia et Umbria* and administered by a governor with the title of *Corrector* who resided at Florence. It underwent another transformation in the second half of the IV century A.D. when *Tuscia* (as it was now called) was divided into two parts, the *Suburbicaria* to the south of the Arno and the *Annonaria* to the north of the river, under a *Consularis*.

CIVILISATION.

The Etruscans made the most of the various sources of wealth belonging to their territory. They gave great importance to agriculture and their lands were largely cultivated, while the iron and copper mines of the Island of Elba, Val di Cecina and Campigliese, furnished them with an abundant supply of raw material not only for industry but also for commerce which they engaged in actively, first with the Phoenicians, then, from the VI century onwards, with the Ionian Greeks. The extent of their commercial relations by sea and by land is proved by the numerous series of coins belonging to the different cities. These first consisted of pieces of rudely shaped bronze; then, passing through intermediate stages, they evolved into a regular system of coinage, in gold, silver and bronze, marked with the symbols of their value, and with emblems which were often of high artistic merit.

Besides the coins, several series of Etruscan weights have also come down to us and a bronze balance similar to those still in use (Chiusi, Civic Museum), with the different weights notched upon the beam and a running weight in the shape of a leaden ball.

Of the extraordinary ability of the Etruscans as architects we shall speak in Part III of this work, in connection with walls and tombs. We will here mention their skill in hydraulic works, which is attested by two surviving monuments, the *Ponte Sodo* on the Cremera and the *Tagliata Etrusca* (Etruscan Channel or Cutting) at Ansedonia.

They were also eminent in the art of medicine, a science allied to a certain extent with their religious beliefs and therefore not exempt from a basis of superstitious magic. And they were masters of odontology, to judge by the sets of teeth with gold fillings that have been discovered in their tombs.

We are, unfortunately, unable to judge of their literary activity, except so far as it is mentioned by Roman writers, for absolutely none of their works have come down to us. Varro mentions Volnius, a writer of Etruscan tragedies; Horace tells us of the Fescennine verses, or popular peasant songs (so called from *Fescennium,* an Etruscan city which has not been definitely identified), which were afterwards introduced into Rome; they seem to have used liturgical chants accompanied by the sound of pipes in their religious rites, and lastly, there were the famous sacred books of the « Etruscan discipline » to which we shall refer more fully in the following chapter.

As for their prose, Varro quotes a passage which speaks of « Etruscan Histories ». We know no more!

Our knowledge of Etruscan music is a little more extensive, thanks chiefly to the mural paintings in their tombs. The sound of the *tibiae* or double pipes, would seem to have been a necessary accompaniment of all ceremonies, sacred and profane, and the skill of Etruscan flautists became proverbial not only in Rome but also in Greece. Their trumpeters and citharists were equally famous.

With such a deep love of music it is only natural that they should have also been devoted to dancing which often assumed a religious or symbolic character as in their war-dance. This is a subject constantly seen in their sepulchral paintings and we will return to it in Part III.

The Etruscans, like the Romans, were greatly addicted to the use of mineral baths and to the practice of gymnastic exercises but more as an amusement than with the object of attaining to perfect physical development, like the Greeks. We notice the same difference of outlook in the Etruscan theatre, especially in the gladiatorial games and, taking into account the general relaxation of manners and customs which became more marked after the IV century B. C., and the women's love of jewellery and rich attire which is clearly revealed by the innumerable figured monuments that have been brought to light, we are justified in coming to the conclusion that the Etruscans, especially in their latest period, became more and more inclined to the material pleasures of life. At the same time we must not forget that Etruria was permeated by Hellenic civilisation, the sum of all the different pre-hellenic civilisation which had flourished on the coasts of the Aegean Sea, and that, while drawing to herself only what she needed, as suited to her native tastes and disposition, she passed Greek culture on to Rome which, without this influence exercised continually from the dawn of her history, might never have been capable, later on, of becoming in her turn, the universal heir of Hellas.

RELIGION.

Tages, a wondrous youth with the wisdom of age who sprang, according to legend, from the fresh-ploughed furrows of Tarquinii, was the reputed teacher of Tarchon the Tarquinian hero, who displayed such extraordinary wisdom even from his childhood that he is said to have been born with a hoary head. Tarchon learnt from Tages the mysteries of haruspicy, the science that taught how to read the divine will in the smoking entrails of animals offered in sacrifice. The famous Tagetic Books contained all the intricate rules of this rite, while the Vegonic or « Thunder » Books preserved the ritual taught by the nymph Vecu (*Vegoe*), perhaps of Chiusi, for interpreting the sacred will as manifested in the thunder-bolts hurled by the nine Great Gods, each of whom was lord of one *manubia,* while Tinia (Jove) alone had the right of wielding three. A special class of priests, named *fulguriatores,* were set apart for the interpretation of the thunder-bolts and they had the power of modifying or limiting their consequences, by the use of a complicated ritual.

The Ritual Books contained minute and complicated instructions for the foundation of cities, the building and orientation of temples, for land-surveying, the subdivision of citizens and the interpretation of prodigies (*ostenta*) and natural phenomena through the answers given by the augurs or piests furnished with a curved wand called *lituus*, and finally, all general laws relating to peace and war. Lastly the Books of Fate preserved the doctrine concerning the destinies of mankind and of the world, while the Acherontic Books (*sacra Acheruntia*, also attributed to Tages) treated of the destinies of life beyond the grave.

This « Etruscan Discipline » or divinatory religion of the Etruscans, was codified about the II century B.C. and translated into Latin by Tarquinius Priscus and others. The Romans continued to turn for centuries, with unabated faith, to these Tarquinian Books of which unfortunately not a vestige has come down to us, with the exception of the fragment of an Acherontic Book which has been indentified in the writing on the twelve linen wrappings of an Egyptian mummy of the Hellenistic era, discovered at Alexandria in Egypt, and now in the Agram Museum. Of the ancient writers, Cicero supplies us with the most information on these subjects.

The three great deities who had temples in every Etruscan city were *Tinia* (Iupiter), *Uni* (Iuno), and *Menrva* (Minerva). They formed a celestial Triad corresponding to the Capitoline Triad of Rome. Their names and those of the other Etruscan divinities are known to us through a very rare and singular bronze relic of the III century B.C. Shaped like a sheep's liver, it is known as the « liver of Piacenza » from having been found at Settima near that city and preserved in the Piacenza Museum. It symbolises « the celestial temple » and divided into so many compartments each containing the name of a deity dominating the corresponding ideal subdivision of the heavenly sphere. The haruspices made use of this curious monument in interpreting the will of the Gods on the liver of the victim. The extensive use of haruspicy in Chaldea, in Babylon and among the Hittites would seem to place the Etruscans in kinship with oriental nations and there are not lacking those who use this argument as an element in favour of their Asiatic origin.

The celestial Triad had its counterpart in the dread Triad of the infernal regions, *Mantus* (*Liberus* or *Bacchus*), *Mania* (*Persephone*) and the Latin goddess *Ceres* who also had a temple dedicated to her in Rome.

Other divinities of whom the names have been transmitted to us were venerated locally in certain cities and associated with the elements of nature: such were *Tiv* (the moon), *Usil* (the sun), *Thesan* (Aurora).

The long, double archaic inscription engraved spirally on a thin, convex metal plate, which was found at Magliano in Tuscany, would also seem to have had a religious character.

Taken as a whole, we cannot give the Etruscan religion credit for marked originality in the creation of its gods which are to be found under modified or different names, among the Pre-Greeks, the Greeks and the Italic tribes and later in Rome. Thus *Phuphluns* answers to Dionysus and Bacchus, *Sethlans* to Haephaestus and Vulcan, *Turms* to Hermes and Mercury, *Turan* to Aphrodite and Venus. Very evident is the affinity of *Maris* with Ares and Mars, of *Nethuns* with Poseidon and Neptune, of *Aplu* with Apollo, of *Artume* with Artemis, of *Hercle* with Hercules and *Ani* with Ianus, who was perhaps originally called *Culsans.*

Vertumnus (Velthurnia) was the god of agriculture and especially connected with vineyards in which capacity he may be compared to the Greek Dionysus and the Roman and Italic Bacchus or Liber. Homage was paid to him every year at his famous shrine the *fanum Voltumnae,* where the Princes of the Confederated Cities of southern Etruria used to meet in solemn conclave for the celebration of rites that were both religious and political.

The goddess of destiny, *Nortia,* corresponding to the Roman Fortuna, was venerated at *Volsinii* (*novi*) and in this city the representatives of the Etruscan cities continued to meet, even under the Empire, for the worship of Vertumnus.

There were also demi-gods and genii. Female demons connected with the mythological cycle of *Turan* (Aphrodite) are frequently seen on bronze mirrors after the IV century, B.C. They were called *Lasae,* and appear as winged figures, nude but with sandals on their feet and adorned with necklaces and diadems. Infernal demons, of both sexes, also having their counterparts in the Greek Hades, as, for instance, the three Parcae, are represented with increasing frequency from the IV century onwards, as terror of the next world became a more marked characteristic of the pleasure-loving Etruscans. They are generally winged figures bearing a torch or a hammer, the material symbol of the inevitability of death which is always treacherous even when natural. The hammer or mallet is also, possibly, a survival of primitive customs.

Foremost among these demons were *Charun,* whose characteristics differ from those of the Greek Charon who is, however, practically his counterpart; *Tuchulcha,* perhaps the generic name of a cruel and monstrous type, and *Phersu* (lat. *persona* = mask), a malevolent, avenging genius. We often find animals depicted in sepulchral paintings and sculptures, and some of them, such as the diabolic horse, the wolf and the serpent, are obviously connected with Etruscan beliefs about life beyond the grave.

In contrast with the infernal demons, there were also wingend genii of a mild and benign nature, precursors of the angels of the Christian religion.

But Greek mythology had so much influence on the Etruscan mind that, in studying their figured monuments, it is not always easy to distinguish what the artist has taken from Greek models and what he has added as being peculiar to specifically Etruscan beliefs. The two elements appear together in the same scene and we often find incidents from the Odyssey or the Heraclean cycle introduced with elaborate variations and wealth of detail.

It is a matter of discussion to what extent Etruscan conceptions of the other world, especially those connected with the deification of souls, were influenced by the Orphic or Phythagoric doctrines which, after the IV century, B.C., exercised a strong influence over various Italic races — above all, over the Oscans — and also on Rome. They do not seem, however, to have affected any radical change in indigenous beliefs.

The calendar employed by the Etruscans was the proto-type of the Roman calendar, with its minute division into lucky and unlucky days. They calculated time on the eastern system, that is by the phases of the moon, not by the course of the sun, and the division of the month was based on the Ides, corresponding to the full moon and indicating the period of eight days during which the Kings of Etruria held audiences and exercised other public functions, and when markets were held. Other complex ceremonies relating to the computation of time and preserved in Rome, find their natural origin and explanation in the Etruscan ritual.

Generally speaking we cannot but recognise in the religious conception of the Etruscans an exaggerated notion and terror of evil, an absolute contrast to the Hellenic conception which tended towards the idealisation of good. That the sacerdotal caste, initiated into the mysteries of the complex ritual, was regarded with great awe and veneration, is clear from the information we derive from Roman sources, for Rome continued for a long period to make an exclusive use of Etruscan priests and especially of Etruscan haruspices, just as she adopted various sacrifical and propitiatory ceremonies of which the Etruscan origin is evident.

II

THE ETRUSCAN LANGUAGE

The Etruscan language has come down to us in about 12.000 inscriptions, mostly consisting of only a few words, which have been discovered over so wide an extension of territory as to offer material for useful investigations into the Etruscans' sphere of activity and their commercial relations with other races. The greater part of these inscriptions were found in Etruria Proper, especially in the southern and eastern districts, in the territory of Chiusi and Tarquinii, but Umbria has also yielded a certain number of epigraphs, chiefly from localities like Todi, nearest to the Etruscan boundaries. Across the Apennines, the district round Bologna has given us various inscriptions, especially since the discovery of Marzabotto, and of the famous bilingual inscription of the haruspex of Pesaro which was found among isolated monuments, on the east coast of Italy. The linguistic forms of an inscription found at Novilara offer no slight resemblance to those of the Etruscans.

In the north-west of Italy, an inscription found at Busca, near Saluzzo (Piedmont) was wrongly held by Mommsen to be of doubtful authenticity. A group of epigraphs found

CHIUSI, Museum. *Stone sphinx.*

in the north were judged at once, from their appearance, to be Etruscan and were definitely recognised as such, after careful investigation, by Pauli. Among them we may mention the Treviso inscription (Valtellina), and those of Voltino on the Lake of Garda and of Rotzo near Bassano. To these must be added the inscriptions written in what Pauli calls the Bolzano alphabet, which were discovered in the Valley of the Adige between Verona and Matrey near Innsbruck. There are also those who see indications of the Etruscans in certain names with the suffix -*enna* which, according to them, would represent a fossilized trace of vanished strata of Etruscan inhabitants, as for instance, in the name of the Rhaetian city of Clavenna, now Chiavenna.

On the west, the sea put a barrier to the extensions of the Etruscan language, although traces of Etruscan names have been found even in Sardinia.

Turning to the south, we find traces of Etruscan linguistic influence in some Faliscan inscriptions, and it is certain, in any case, that the political and linguistic sphere of the Etruscan people extended at one time from the territory of Rome to Campania. The longest, or one of the longest, inscriptions was discovered at Capua and others were brought to light at Suessola. Lastly it would seem that onomastic and epigraphic traces of the Etruscans have been found both in Calabria and in Sicily.

The Etruscans left written records of themselves beyond the borders of Italy. One of the most remarkable is inscribed on the linen wrappings of an Egyptian mummy, to which we will return shortly. An Etruscan mirror was also discovered in Egypt, and at Carthage, an ivory tablet with

FLORENCE, Archaeological Museum. Ivory tablet with phoenician-greek alphabet (from right to left). From Marsiliana.

Etruscan words, perhaps a dedication to Melkart. Most important of all is the Stone of Lemnos, inscribed with two epigraphs which, some dissentients notwithstanding, are considered by many scholars to be, in their linguistic forms, very similar to the Etruscan idiom.

* * *

Partial collections of Etruscan inscriptions had been in existence for some time when at Turin, in 1867, Ariodante Fabretti gave « a generally correct codification of the Etruscan language » in his *Corpus Inscriptionarum Italicarum*, kept up to date by three *Supplements* until 1878 and by an *Appendix* written by Gamurrini, in 1880.

These texts were revised by C. Pauli, with the assistance of O. A. Danielsson and incorporated with fresh material in a *Corpus Inscriptionum Etruscarum,* of which the first volume (Leipzig, 1893-1902) includes northern Etruria with about 5000 inscriptions. The publication of the second volume, after the death of Pauli, was undertaken by Danielsson, aided by A. Torp, G. Herbig, B. Nogara. The first part includes Orvieto and Bolsena, Populonia, Vetulonia, Sovana, Magliano, Veii; Tarquinia; the second (1907 ss.) part contains the inscriptions of the Faliscan and Capuan territory (n. 8001-8600); while a supplement gives the long inscription on the Agram mummy wrappings; other parts are now published or in preparation.

* * *

A brief enumeration of the longest and most important inscriptions must naturally begin with the writing on the famous mummy wrappings preserved in the Agram Museum, and published in 1892 by Krall. It is the unique *manuscript* text which has come to us in Etruscan written on linen. It contains fragments of a liturgical calender. The roll (*volumen*) was then cut into many strips to wrap around the mummy of a woman found in Egypt. It goes back to the Ptolemaic or Roman era (1st century B.C.). There remain only 12 strips of various lengths, that appear to make up about half of the entire book, that would have had a length of about 14 metres, and was divided into exactly 12 columns. The writing is very accurate, in black ink, from the right to the left. With comparatively enormous efforts, putting to use all our internal and external linguistic knowledge, we have been able to interpret more than 500 different words of it, and taking into account the many repetitions, we have reached a total of about 1200 words.

They prescribe various acts of worship, sacrifices and libations, month by month, with many analogies in certain parts, to the contents of another famous epigraphic text of the Umbriam civilisation, the *Tavole iguvine.*

There are named various divinities, among which is the supreme Etruscan god, Tinia, and Neptune.

* * *

The most celebrated inscription on terracotta is the one on the S. Maria di Capia *tile* ascribed to the V century B. C. and now in the Berlin Museum. Notwithstanding the mutilation of the upper and lower corners, it still contains about 300 words. From a hermeneutic point of view, Lattes has pointed out that it presents many coincidences with the

Agram mummy wrappings and with the Piacenza Bronze and he has published an interesting series of studies on the latter monument and the Capua *tile*.

Then there is the famous *cippus* of Perugia, of a late epoch,containing about 120 words which are believed by some to be of a funerary character. Two families are mentioned, *Afuna* and *Velthina,* and there is frequent use of the word *naper* followed by numbers, also found on a cippus at Volterra. It has been conjectured that *naper* indicates some measurement and that the text refers to a division of land between the two families.

An Etruscan inscription of nine lines is scratched on one side of the square pillar in the tomb known as the « Grotta del Tifone » at Tarquinii. It contains the name of the *Pumpa* family (II century B. C.).

The « queen of Etruscan inscriptions » according to Maffei, is the one engraved on the wall of a hypogeum below the Tower of S. Manno, near Perugia. It consists of 28 words, the last one of only two letters, and it refers to the *Precu* family, mentioned also on other monuments.

Among inscriptions of a certain length on sarcophagi, we may mention those of the *Pulena* family at Tarquinii, one of which, written on a roll held by the personage whose sculptured figure adorns the lid, consists of nine lines, and about sixty words, including proper names, words indicating degrees of relationship, offices, etc. Other similar epigraphs, but briefer, are those in the tomb of the *Alethnas* family at Viterbo, and the inscriptions at Toscanella.

The most important inscription on metal is the so-called *Templum* of Piacenza for the which refer to p. 62.

The so-called *Piombo* or *Leaden Plate* of Magliano (VI
century B.C.), inscribed on both sides, must equally have
had some ritual meaning, as the names of gods occur in the
inscription. It is preserved in the Etruscan Museum of
Florence and was illustrated with much erudition by Milani.

In the Guarnacci Museum at Volterra there is a small
leaden plate inscribed with about eighty words (III century
B.C.); and a similar relic, found at Campiglia Marittima,
is now in the Florence Museum. In both cases, the inscriptions would appear to be in the nature of votive prayers
as they cannot be compared with the leaden plates on
sepulchral urns. A gold plate found at Tarquinii and
published by Gamurrini, contains nine lines that some
suppose to have reference to a votive prayer, though others
deny it (Skutsch).

Lastly there is the inscription of *Aulus Metellus* or the
Orator which runs along the border of the *pallium* of a
bronze statue discovered in 1566 near Lake Thrasymene
and preserved in the Florence Museum.

The last great discovery is that of the three gold laminae
found in the shrine dedicated to the godess *Leukothea,* at
Pyrgi (Santa Severa), near the port of Caere (S. Marinella
to the south of Civitavecchia), destined to be riveted on
to a small ligneous table. Two are in Etruscan characters,
but one (and it is the first time that this has occured)
contains if not a proper literal translation, certainly an
editing of the same contents in the Phoenician-Punic
language. Consequently one can consider using a bilingual
method for a true and exact deciphering of the Etruscan.

This lamina has served to confirm the exact meaning of the various words already glimpsed by the more reliable scholars. In the specific instance it tells of a benefit brought to the sovereign of Caere, in Etruscan *Kisria*, Thefarie Velianas (i.e. Tiberius Velianas) by the goddess *Uni* (Giunone), in the Punic text identified with Astarte, and of gifts and ritual acts ordered by the grateful sovereign. The larger Etruscan lamina contains sixteen lines with thirty-six words, the other nine with fifteen. The first adheres to the Punic text (of eleven lines with thirty words). One can date it at about 500 B.C.

New York, Metropolitan Museum.
Etruscan bucchero vase with phoenician-greek alphabet.

The Etruscans had the custom of writing on statues, as on other objects, such as mirrors, domestic utensils, vases, etc. and round painted figures on the walls of tombs.

* * *

There is a controversy about how the Phoenician-Greek alphabet arrived in Etruria. Some hold that it came to the north from Cuma in Campania, others (that I think are right) that it came directly to the Etruscans from Greece and from them descended to the south.

However it pertains to the western group of the Greek alphabets on account of the order of the last three letters added by the Greeks, such as transpires from some archaic alphabets, as for example, those on the upper edge of an eburnean tablet from Marsiliana d'Albegna in Florence, and on the little cockeral-shaped vase from Viterbo, now kept in the Metropolitan Museum in New York. It consists of twenty-six letters. Later, for phonetic requirements, the Etruscans added a twenty-seventh letter, shaped like an 8, and prononced like an *f*, at the end of the alphabet (we also have varieties of it), and viceversa omitted in practice from making use of any letters of the old alphabet. By the V century B.C. the Etruscan alphabet consisted of the following sounds:

vowels: *a i e u*;
consonants: *c* (= *k*) *v z h th l m n p s r ś t ph kh f*.

Rarely used were the *k* and the *q*. Of all the letters, there are missing only the sound *o* and the sonants *b*, *d* and *g*.

As one can see, there were various sibilant signs with numerous nuances, for us not easily or precisely reproduced: the *ś* is used to transcribe the sign *M*.

The simple reading of inscriptions does not now present any difficulties and a knowledge of Graeco-Latin alphabets makes it, generally speaking, an easy task. It is well known that Etruscan writing nearly always goes from right to left, like other ancient Italic inscriptions; later the Etruscans adopted the Roman system of writing from left to right, and between the old and the new method, there was a period of hesitation and uncertainty.

Another peculiarity of Etruscan inscriptions is seen in the so-called *boustrophedon* writing which appears on the famous *tile* of S. Maria di Capua.

There is also the writing known as *spiral* which is seen in the inscription of Barbarano di Sutri and in the epigraph on a piece of pottery in the form of a bird.

The words of Etruscan inscriptions are generally separated by dots; in those of the best period we find two dots used, as in the above-mentioned S. Manno inscription. In the archaic epoch there were three dots, in the most recent, only one: sometimes they are totally lacking.

* * *

It is believed that the most ancient Etruscan inscriptions date from the VII century B. C. Among the oldest are those of Vetulonia, Caere, Barbarano, Narce, etc.

In the more recent inscriptions, such as those on the Agram mummy wrappings, there is a great deal of indecision in the spelling. The bilingual inscriptions and those written in Latin characters are naturally the latest. The latest inscriptions known to us date from the time of Augustus, but it is generally admitted that the Etruscan language continued to exist for several centuries later, if not as a spoken idiom, at any rate in the same way as Sanskrit exists today. Lucretius speaks of *carmina thyrrena* which were read in inverted order, and he speaks of them as of a thing well-known and used in his own day; three hundred years later the haruspices attached to the armies of Julian the Apostate, read their ritual books no less well than those of the time of Cicero, although there are those who believe that they must have made use of Latin translations.

Leaving aside the question of the probable survival of the Etruscan language in ancient and modern dialects, a question on which the learned are by no means agreed, we may mention that Papias and the Suda Dictionary quote Etruscan words, which shows that they must have been acquainted with extracts from writings now lost, containing, in some form or another, specimens of the Etruscan tongue. Papias lived about 1053 and the "Suda" lexicon was compiled under the Emperor Alexis Comnenus. Similar quotations are found in Hesychius and others.

Studies and researches into the Etruscan language were begun by the Romans themselves, and carried on chiefly by Varro and the Emperor Claudius. It is not likely that the Grammarians should have neglected Etruscan, indeed echos of their investigations on the subject can be found in Agratius (IV cent.) where he treats of the sound represented by the letter *s*.

* * *

We do not know if or how these studies were continued in the Middle Ages. It was in the XIV century, according to Maffei, that the first attempts were made to decipher the Etruscan tongue. Perhaps this must be understood in the sense that attempts were made to explain the *glosses* or Etruscan words preserved in classic writers. However this may be, it is a fact that since the days of Annius of Viterbo who published his 17 *Books of Antiquities,* in Rome, in 1498, innumerable efforts have been made to decipher the Etruscan language, first by the so-called *etymological* method and afterwards by the *combinative* method.

The first consists either in starting with the preconceived idea that the Etruscans belonged to one special race and then explaining the glosses and inscriptions in accordance with the language or languages of that race basing the theory chiefly on consonance between Etruscan words and those of the other idiom, or else by starting with the idea of consonance and hunting for languages with words similar in sound of which the meaning may be applied to the Etruscan.

It is needless to say that these attempts have always failed although they have been ardently pursued for over two centuries until the present day, by famous scholars, both in Italy and elsewhere, and it is no exaggeration to say that besides the Semitic, Celtic and Graeco-Italic tongues, nearly every known language has been laid under contribution, not excluding those of the American continent.

Seeing the uselessness of these efforts, W. Deecke, the real founder of scientific Etruscology, published a pamphlet in 1875 in which he maintained that the Etruscan language could only be explained *through itself*; that comparisons with other languages were futile, at any rate, in the present state of our knowledge. With these words Deecke definitely inaugurated the combinative method which he practised himself and which consists in « taking into special examination the shorter inscriptions, known to be of a sepulchral or votive nature, or indicative of definite objects or persons, and comparing them with one another or grouping them in series, removing from each the words signifying proper names of individuals or deities and then endeavouring to grasp the sense of the remaining words by careful study of their collocation or their suffixes which latter would indicate inflections of cases if nouns, or forms of conjugation if verbs » (*Ducati*).

This is the only way that can possibly lead to results, small perhaps but certain, for nothing is more dangerous in the investigation of an unknown tongue than to allow oneself to be carried away by comparisons with other known languages, without any solid basis such as would be supplied by a bilingual text or a text sufficiently extensive to permit of its general meaning being grasped with certainty through the situation or character of the monument on which it is inscribed.

* * *

Deecke's method was taken up by other scholars, including Pauli, Torp, Skutsch, and G. Herbig.

To give some idea of the most notable results obtained by the combinative method, I will give a summary of all that it has hitherto been possible to determine with a fair amount of accuracy, as to the meaning and grammatical forms of a number of Etruscan words.

Let us begin with the grammar:

Masculine nouns end in - *a*, - *e*, - *i*, - *u* and in - *th*, - *n*. Ex. *Vipina* = Vibenna, *Aule* = Aulus, *Senti* = Sentius, *Pumpu* = Pompeius, *Arunth* = Aruns, *clan* = son.

Feminine nouns end in - *a*, - *i*, - *ia*, - *ei*, - *ai*, - *c*, - *l*, - *tha*. Ex. *Menrva* = Minerva, *Hasti* = Fastia, *Velia, puia* = wife, *Elinei, Elinai* = Helena, *sec.* = daughter, *Thanchvil* = Tanaquil, *lautnitha* = liberta (freedwoman).

The plural ends in - *ar*, - *ur*, - *r*. Ex. *clen-ar*, from *clan* - sons, with a vowel change that is also found in certain inflections.

The full form of the suffix would seem to be - *ara* - as in *clen-ara-s'i*. Then we have *thans-ur* from *thans*, *tiv-r* - months, from *tiv* - moon or month; *cape-r* - cups, etc, etc.

As for « cases », there is very little difference between the genitive and the dative. We find forms in *s, s'*. Ex. *Sethre-s* from *Sethre*; *hinthial patrucles* = the shade of Patroclus, *hinthial terasias'* = the shade of Tiresias; *clen-s'* from *clan* = son, dative or genitive *clen-s'i*. In consonant nouns we find - *us*. Ex. *Velthur-us* from *Velthur*.

Another form of the genitive, is *al*. We find it also in the following bilingual inscriptions: *ruvfi-al* = of Rufius, etc.

C.I.E., (1) n. 3763.

p. volumnius a. f. violens cafatia natus   (Latin).

pup velimna au cahatial.   (Etruscan).

C.I.E., n. 714, 715.

ar(nth) spedo thocerual clan   (Etruscan).
Vel Spedo Thoceronia natus   (Latin).

We read on a mirror: *mi thancvilus fulnial* - this (is) of
Tanaquil Fulnia.

Then we have: *arnth-al* = of Aruns, *larth-al* = of Lars,
ruvfi-al = of Rufius, *ruvfi,* etc.

The suffix *al* sometimes forms adjectives, as *truial* =
Trojan. Then there are the characteristc combinations of *s*
and *l*. They are used for the so-called *genitivus genitivi,* or
double genitive. We have a characteristic example in a
Tarquinian inscription: *trepi tranchvil vipenas arnthal*
arthialis'la puia, which evidently means: Tanaquil Trebia
wife of Aruns Vibenna (son) of Aruns, or Aruntes. The
form *arnthal arnthialis'la* is the genitive of *arnth arnthial.*

Various suffixes of the locative case have also been
identified: the most certain is - *ti* - *thi*. Ex. *cela-ti* = in
the cell; *tarchnai-thi* = in Tarquinii.

The termination - *ach* indicates origin or ethnical source.
Ex. *cneve tarchu rumach* = Gnaivos Tarquinius romanus;
velznach = volsiniensis, etc. The termination - *na* indicates
pertinence. Ex. *suthina* = sepulchral.

We also have the pronoun *mi* = I; *e-ca, ce-n, ce-he-n*
= this, and the demonstrative adverb *thu-i* = here.

There are two Etruscan *conjunctions* corresponding to
the Latin - *que*: - *c* and - *m,* or *um.* Ex. *av(le ale)thnas (a)*
rnthal clan thanchvilus ruvfial... = Aulus Alethnas of Aruns
son and of Tanaquil Rufia.

Arnth leinies larthial clan velusum nefis... = Aruns
Leinies of Lartius son and of Velius grandson.

We know very little about Etruscan *verbs*. The characteristic perfect tenses in *-ce* are very numerous and were identified long ago. Ex. *am-ce* = was; *ar-ce* = did; *tur-ce, tur-u-ce* = gave; *lup-u-ce* = died; *sval-ce* = lived; *tham-ce* = built, etc.

There are others ending simply in *- u*. Ex. *tur-u* = gave; *lup-u* = died; there would seem to be still others ending in *- ne* as *mul-u-ne* = built, had made; *tu-ru-ne* = gave, etc.

Lastly I must mention the past participles in *- i-l,* used in the passive sense, as *ac-i-l* = held, *vac-i-l* = said; and the participles or active gerunds in *-as,* as *sval-th-as* = having lived, as against *sval-ce* = lived; *zilachn-th-as* = having filled the office of *zilath.*

As for the numerals, the inscribed dicos and other epigraphic elements allow us with almost certainty to be able to establish the following succession: 1 = *thu,* 2 = *zal,* 3 = *ci,* 4 = *sa,* 5 = *mach,* 6 = *huth,* or according to others: 4 = *mach,* 5 = *sa,* nevertheless *sa* is not = 6. After, to conjecture, perhaps 7 = *cezp,* 8 = *semph* (or viceversa), 9 = *nurph,* 10 = *muiaph* (or = 7) or perhaps *sar.*

Words indicating degrees of relationship:

clan = son. *puia* = wife. *prumaths'* = great grandson. *sec* = daughter. *nefis'* = grandson. *lautn* = family. *lautn-i* = freedman. *lautni-tha* = freedwoman.

Words of a sepulchral meaning:

hinthial = shade, soul. *suthi* = tomb, hypogeum. *suthi' na* = sepulchral. *capra* = coffin. *murs'* = ossuary. *thaura* = urn or sarcopragus. *cela* = cell.

Words of different meanings:

usil = sun; *tiv* = moon or month; *fleres* = statue; *phersu* = mask (latin *persona*).

Words relative to public offices:

maruna = aedilis (?), *zilath* = praetor (?), *zilath mech-lum rasnas* = princeps (praetor) Etruriae, *camthi* = camillus (?), *purth* = dictator (?).

Words relative to social strata: *lautni* = familiar, freedman; *eterav* = slave.

Verbal terms:

am-ce = was. *sval-ce* = lived. *lup-u-ce* = died. *arce* = did. *ter-ce* = placed, dedicated. *tur-ce* = offered, gave. *zichu-che* = wrote. *tham-ce* = built. *mu-lu, mul-u-ne* = built, had made. *ten-u* = acted, etc.

* * *

Although there can be no doubt about the value and superiority of the *combinative* method as compared with the *etymological* method, we are forced to confess that its results have gradually been growing scantier and that so far from giving us the key to the Etruscan language, it has not even enabled us to state its nature with any certainty or to determine its relation to any one group of languages. To form an exact idea of the present state of the question, it must be remembered that during the last few years two principal schools of *serious* researches have arisen, the one of a purely *philological* character, while the other we may describe as *philological-hermeneutic.* We omit all mention of other attempts of various kinds that, for one reason or another, do not deserve to be taken into serious consideration.

* * *

Given the scanty results obtained by the *combinative* method to which we have already referred, some scholars have returned to a rigorous application of Pauli's rule: *Study the Etruscan language through itself,* and leaving aside, for the present at any rate, all hermeneutic theories, they are concentrating their efforts solely on the characteristics of the Etruscan language as they result very clearly from philological investigations into the words of the mysterious inscriptions. In this way it becomes easier, first to ascertain the actual nature of Etruscan itself and then to trace its relationship to other linguistic groups.

The most distinguished name in the history of this branch of studies is undoubtedly that of Gustave Herbig who has always affirmed that the Etruscan language can only be compared to itself: *Etruscan with Etruscan.* His writings are full of acute epigraphic, phonetic and morphological arguments all tending to show how study of Etruscology can be assisted by a rigorous application of the method of Indo-Germanic glossology.

From material put together by Schulze for the study of Etrusco-Latin onomatology and by Sundwall for the study of Asiatic onomatology (1913), Herbig compiled in 1914 an orderly though provisional comparison between Asia and Etruria, arranging the names in two lists according to identity of suffixes with different roots or variations of suffix with one single root. The conclusion of Herbig's acute research is that there is a close connection between Asiatic and Etruscan idioms both as regards phonetics, suffixes and roots.

The valuable work of the learned professor of Munich has been ably continued by Eva Fiesel. In her work: *Das grammatische Geschlecht im Etruskischen* (Göttingen, 1922) she examines the question as to whether or not Etruscan belongs to those languages that admit a difference of grammatical gender, strictly according to Herbig's method.

Eva Fiesel comes to the conclusion that in the most ancient period there was no precise distinction between masculine and feminine nouns and that it is only in the later inscriptions that we find nouns of the feminine gender ending in *-i* and *-ia*, as *arnthia, caia, fastia,* etc. This sexualisation of the old Etruscan suffix *-i* applied indifferently to either gender, was probably due to the influence exercised by the Latin language over the Etruscan between the VI and V centuries B. C.

Ribezzo does not accept the authoress' conclusions, observing that however much literary usages may be lacking, a language does not undergo any substantial change in the course of one or two centuries, with the exception of a certain partial phonetic development and of the introduction or disuse of some secondary forms. He quotes as examples the *Cippus* of the Forum and the Dueno inscription. The superimposition of new suffixes indicative of sex on to the old Italic feminine form of *-i,* which undoubtedly took place in the VI and V centuries, is, according to Ribezzo, an eloquent proof that the Etruscans were settled in Etruria long before 800 B.C.

* * *

Turning now to the other category of researches of a

hermeneutic or *philological-hermeneutic* character, of which we have already spoken, we must keep in mind first of all the series of scientific comparisons initiated by Thomsen in 1899 between the Etruscan language and those of the Caucasic group. Trombetti revised these researches in 1908 and completed them with a large amount of fresh material, in his Memoir *On the Affinities of the Etruscan language,* which was followed in 1912 by another Memoir with the same title.

Trombetti's conclusions are as follows:

1. That the Etruscan language is more akin to the Indo-European and Caucasic than to any other linguistic group;

2. That it is more akin to the Caucasic than to the Indo-European.

The Etruscan language, however, does not form part of either the Indo-European or the Caucasic families, but belongs, together with the primitive languages of Asia Minor, « to an intermediate group between the Indo-European and the Caucasic ». It is not astonishing, says Trombetti, that Etruscan should be akin to both the Indo-European and Caucasic families, because these two linguistic groups are connected with one another.

Today however a third method is prefered on account of its excellent results, already proved on a large scale, and that is the method which takes into consideration the close pairs of words and expressions between Etruscan and Latin inscriptions, with identical or very similar meaning. Naturally one must be sure that the two epigraphs reflect analogous situations and concepts. Such is the case above all of the funeral inscriptions with the *cursus*

honorum, that is to say with the very fixed succession of
the public offices. This is the system called « historical-
cultural » or « historical-religious ».

By now the majority of the scholars (one must not
take into account the dilettanti amongst whom there is
no one of culture or learning) think that the Etruscan
language belongs to a para— or pre-Indo-European belt,
that is to say with a base not Indo-European, but with
considerable borrowings that eventually occured over the
years, pertaining itself however to an area very close to
the Indo-European. Later, of note, were the acquisitions
of words from the Latin and the Umbrian.

Important analogies between the Etruscan and the
Lydian languages have been noted in Littmann's work on
the bilingual inscriptions discovered at Sardis (published in
1916) especially as regards enclitics and the determination
of the genitive and other cases, as Trombetti has also
acknowledged in his Glossology (1922).

After the publication of Hrozny's book: « Die Sprache
der Hethiter » (1917), analogies were also traced between
the Etruscan and the Hittite tongues.

However this may be, it must be admitted that up to
the present day neither the Lydian nor the Hittite tongue
has given us the greatly desired key to the Etruscan
language. And the same may be said for another attempt
made, though from a different point of view, to connect
the Etruscan language with the ancient idioms of Asia
Minor.

In a work published in Greek at Athens, in 1912,
Jacob Thomopulos, with an abundance of material taken

from ancient glossaries and inscriptions in Asia Minor
and other regions, attempts to prove that the modern
Albanian language is the best key for deciphering the ancient
idioms both of Asia Minor and Etruria, because, according
to him, the populations of Asia Minor, the Lycians, Carians
and Lydians, like the Hittites, the Tyrrhenians of Italy and
of Lemnos, the Cretans, etc., all spoke languages akin to
one another. The idea of the Albanian language as a
connecting-link is not new. Blau had already used it to
explain the Lycian.

* * *

The second category of researches that we have just
been discussing includes the theory of the « italianissimi »
as Skutsch used to call it, the theory, that is, of those who
hold that Etruscan is not only an Aryan idiom but essentially
and absolutely an Italic idiom. The most distinguished
exponent of this school was the late Elia Lattes who for
more than fifty years (1869-1925) devoted himself whole-
heartedly to the study of the Etruscan problem and
especially to that of the Etruscan language.

* * *

Bartolomeo Nogara was an authoritative follower of
Lattes. He has done much good work for Etruscology, not
least of which is his valued collaboration in the *Corpus
Inscriptionum Etruscarum*. He too, « my illustrious disci-
ple » as Lattes wrote of him in 1919, has remained faithful,
though with certain reservations, to the Italian origin of
Etruscan.

* * *

But some scholars (such as Coli and Pavano) continue to persist in examining the Etruscan alone or with other Indo-European languages, and propound translations based on the arbitary division of words by finding the Greek root in them, arriving at translations completely lacking in good sense.

Amongst the living scholars who are directly occupied with the Etruscan language (and obviously the epigraphs as well) we remember C. Battisti, G. Devoto, J. Heurgon, M. Lejeune, K. Olzscha, M. Pallottino, A. J. Pfiffig, to whom are added various disciples in the field of scientific affirmation.

* * *

What yet remains to be done for the decipherment of the Etruscan language? Buonamici wrote in the first edition of this Guide (1926):

« Our choice is limited, it lies between resignation and perseverance. We must either wait patiently for the discovery of some bilingual or other monument capable of giving us the exact meaning of a certain number of words or inscriptions, or we must continue to fight with the only weapon that can be of any real use, i.e. with the *combinative* method, controlled and directed by happy flashes of intuition such as may guide us in applying the results already obtained and in making further progress on the same lines. If in the future, excavations are carried on more intensively than in the past, we may hope for the discovery either of bilingual inscriptions or, at any rate, of epigraphs of a certain length, of which we could use the contexts to further the application of the combinative method, as was done for the Umbrian language through the study of the Eugubine Tables ».

HANNOVER, Kestner Museum. *Bronze Centaur.*

III

ART

ORIGIN AND GENERAL FEATURES.

While admitting that Etruscan art was influenced by Greek models, it is now fully recognised that it also had a rich life of its own, with a distinctive national character; and if it was sometimes lacking in inventiveness and the aesthetic sense, it had a marked individuality, differentiating it from every other kind of contemporary art. A strong sense of realism gave Etruscan art an outstanding primacy in portraiture, with a tendency to accentuate bodily movements and expressions; it exercised a powerful and lasting influence on the art of Rome which also owed to Etruria the principle of the arch, the construction of fortresses, bridges, acqueducts, temples, etc.

The origin of Etruscan art is to be sought in the simple, unpretentious, geometrical designs belonging to the proto Etruscan civilisation of the iron age known as *Villanovian* (X - VIII cent. B. C.). This perhaps owed to the Etruscans or to commercial contacts its gradual transformation into a civilisation of an oriental type, characterised by the abundance of objects (jewellery, scarabaei, and articles of bronze, iron, silver-gilt, ivory and amber) of a Phoenician-Cypriot and Egyptian character, found in tombs of this period which corresponds to the end of the VIII and the whole of the VII century B. C.

One characteristic of Etruscan art is that every important centre has its own particular type, which makes it easier to analyse each branch separately than to form a comprehensive synthesis of the evolution of their united artistic activities, which indeed it is very hard to trace. We can, however, on general lines, divide Etruscan art into two periods: the first or archaic period, extending from the VII to the V century B.C.; the second, from the IV to the beginning of the I century B. C., and in this latter period are included both the full development and the rapid decadence of Etruscan art.

ARCHITECTURE.

a) *Civil Architecture.*

Etruscan cities were generally built on elevated sites and founded in accordance with certain strict, unvarying rites and ceremonies; at a period certainly not earlier than the V century, B. C., they were surrounded by massive walls, sometimes constructed of enormous, unhewn, polygonal stones, a type traditionally known as «Cyclopean» or «Pelasgic» (ex. *Saturnia*), or of smoothed stones (ex. *Ansedonia*); others consisted of almost quadrangular blocks

The walls of Bolsena (*Volsinii*)

VULCI, *Etrusco - Roman bridge of the Abbadia.*

(ex. *Roselle, Cortona, Vetulonia, Volterra, Populonia*); others again were squared and set up in more or less regular courses of a pseudo-isodomon and isodomon type (ex. *Fiesole*), the choice being apparently guided by the material at hand and the natural position, so that it is hardly possible to place them in strict chronological order.

The walls were completed with towers and broken by gates, the latter never being less than three in number. At Volterra in the *Porta all'Arco* (III-II cent. B. C., but in part of a later date) we have the application of the double arch. Of a still later period are the two gates of Perugia, the *Porta Marzia,* and the *Arch of Augustus*; the latter belongs to the Roman epoch and has curious decorations above the archivolt.

There is only one example of a brick wall in Etruria and that is at Arezzo. In many sites considerable portions of the ancient walls are still in perfect preservation, giving an excellent idea of the way the cities were fortified against enemy attacks.

As we said above, the building of Etruscan cities was regulated by religious rules and carried out according to certain fixed principles. The straight streets intersecting one another at right angles correspond to the Roman *cardini* when they went from north to south, and *decumani* when they lay from east to west. The largest central thoroughfares each way correspond respectively on either side and a complete system of drainage existed in the subsoil.

The houses, of modest proportions, were grouped round a central courtyard furnished with a well; those of the better class had an *atrium* (the typical *atrium tuscanicum* which afterwards became common in Rome) with a gutter for rainwater (*impluvium*) and a large space at the back of the *atrium* called the *tablinum.* The roof either sloped towards the centre (*compluvium*) or outwardly (*displuvium*) or it might be a terraced roof. The houses were generally built of wood faced with terracotta. The remains of foundations can still be seen within the area of Etruscan cities excavated near *Marzabotto* (Bologna) and *Vetulonia* (Grosseto).

7.

VOLTERRA - *Porta all'Arco.*

Many ancient sewers date back to the Etruscans and if the *cloaca maxima* at Rome, as we see it now, is certainly of Roman origin, except the interior blocks in the outlet on the river Tevere, the *cloaca* still partially preserved at Porto S. Clementino would seem to be Etruscan work of a late period.

There are no bridges of which it can be unhesitatingly asserted that they were built by the Etruscans but we are

FLORENCE, Archaeological Museum. *House-urn.*

perhaps not wrong in attributing to them the *Ponte del Bulicame* at *Viterbo,* the *Ponte della Rocca* near Bieda and the bridge crossing the Cremera at Veii. The *Ponte Sodo,* also at Veii and the *Tagliata* at Ansedonia are eloquent witnesses to the grand hydraulic works for which the Etruscans were famous.

b) *Temples.*

The Etruscan or Tuscanic type of temple was, as we have said, afterwards adopted by the Romans and, more or less, by the other peoples of the Peninsula, so that it is also called the Italic temple.

As a rule, only the foundations were of stone; the *cella* or body of the edifice was of sun-dried bricks, the trabeation and the columns, of wood. Such buildings were easily destroyed by fire and no Etruscan temple properly so called has come down to us, though the foundations of temples can be studied in late examples at *Marzabotto* (Bologna), where the remains of the ancient city came to light, also at *Orvieto,* at *Veii* and in the *Faliscan* and *Latian* territories.

The temple was composed of an anterior portico with smooth Tuscanic columns, each set on a cylindrical plinth and with a shaft narrowing slightly as it approached the Doric capital; and of a closed area either containing one single *cella* or subdivided into three divisions, dedicated to the triad of Etruscan deities corresponding to Iupiter, Iuno and Minerva. The whole building followed certain exact laws of orientation and proportion, laws which have been transmitted to us by Vitruvius and which can be verified in such remains of temples as still exist and in the most ancient Etrusco-Roman temples (*Fiesole*).

Of this type was the archaic Roman temple dedicated to *Ceres, Liberus* and *Libera* (beginning of V cent. B. C.); while the most sacred shrine of ancient Rome, the great temple of Iupiter Capitolinus, of which the original construction is said to date from the days of the Tarquinii, was nothing but an Etruscan temple. It was for this sanctuary that the artist *Vulca* of *Veii* executed the famous terracotta statue of Jupiter, and the chariot surmounting the pediment was also the work of Veientine sculptors.

BERLIN, Antiquarium.
Decoration in terracotta from a temple in Caere.

CAERE - *Regolini-Galassi tomb* (Photo Alinari).

a)

Terracotta antefixae from Caere:
a) PARIS, Louvre.

b) BERLIN, Antiquarium.

b)

* * *

Polychrome terracotta decorations formed a characteristic feature of Etrusco-Italic temples and we are fortunate in possessing so many examples of this art that we are able to study them thoroughly in all their different styles and methods of application. We can but feel unbounded admiration for the minute care and technical ability displayed by these Italic craftsmen who, even if they drew their inspiration from Greek art, yet managed to stamp their productions with a typically indigenous touch. Our examples come chiefly from *Cerveteri* and the *Faliscan* and *Latian* territories, only later (III-II cent.) from *Luni* and from *Talamone.*

Three phases are to be distinguished: the first, dating from about the middle and end of the VI century B. C., gives us specimens of terminal pediment tiles and of tiles belonging to friezes of the trabeation; the second phase, from the end of the VI century to about the middle of the V century, is marked by the use of paler clay and greater variety of decoration, which now includes figures as well as ornamental designs; the third phase — following a period of interruption of over a century which is also noticeable in other branches of Etruscan art — lasted from the end of the IV to the first decades of the II century and we perceive in it two predominant tendencies, one naturalistic and the other archaistic. In all three phases there is considerable variation in the application of polychromy and in the choice of subjects.

The terminal roof beams of the façades of temples were also decorated (*antefixae*), as well as the cornice and apex

The roof of the Tomb at Quinto Fiorentino.

COMEANA (Florence) - *The roof of the Montefortini tomb.*

CAERE - *Circular tumuli in the Etruscan necropolis.*

of pediments (*acroteria*) and the ends of roofing tiles, with a variety of ornaments such as stags, griffins, knights and horses, gorgons, chariots and warriors, amazons, maenads, sileni, etc. etc. Great terracotta groups were also placed on the roof over particular supports.

From the IV century onwards complex terracotta groups also fill the tympanum and at this period stone buildings begin to make their appearance.

A chamber of an Etruscan tomb in Populania

* * *

c) *Tombs.*

Circular tombs and chamber-tombs are found sporadically in the midst of well-tombs containing cineary urns, and burial-tombs where the body was either laid in the ground or placed in a coffin. During the whole period of Etruscan domination the two rites, cremation and inhumation, were practised alternately, according to local tradition or conditions, until in the decadent period cremation finally prevailed, under Roman influence.

Therefore in some tombs we find niches for cinerary urns; in others low stone benches ranged against the walls for the reception of bodies; in others again recesses in the walls to contain sepulchral couches, the four sides being grooved to allow for the legs, or the recesses themselves were hewn out in the form of couches with double cushions, carved and painted.

The chamber-tombs were sometimes excavated in the soil and then they are more properly called *hypogeums*, as that of the *Volumni* near Perugia, one of the best preserved; sometimes they were constructed level with the ground and then covered with earth heaped up and cultivated or grass-sown so as to give the appearance of natural tumuli, which are variously known as *meloni* at Cortona, *montarozzi* at Tarquinii, *cuccumelle* at Vulci. Those of the later period were supported and kept together by a *crepido* or low circular base of masonry.

Tombs were of various shapes, either circular like those near Quinto Fiorentino and at Casal Marittimo, or quadrangular, often with spandrils at the corners to create the effect of a pseudo-cupola, effected by closing in the roof with gradually narrowing stone courses ending in a keystone (*Populonia, Vetulonia,* etc.).

The oldest chamber-tomb is the Grotta *Regolini-Galassi* at Cervéteri (*Caere*) which, from the oriental type of its contents, can be attributed to the VII century B. C. A peculiar construction found in this and other tombs, consists in an attempt at an arch formed by the gradual convergence of the stone wall-blocks which are not, however, carried up to a point but terminate in an empty space roofed over with horizontal blocks, either fitting accurately into the sides or simply laid across. This is the pseudo-vault formed on an acute angle, of which we find the exact counterpart in the Creto-Mycenaean civilisation, two thousand years before the Christian era.

A type of tomb entirely excavated in the soil was in use from the VI century onwards. It consisted of one or more rectangular chambers, sometimes with pilasters and columns supporting the flat roof which was either plain or coffered. We find tombs of this kind at *Cerveteri, Tarquinii, Orvieto, Cortona* and elsewhere. Tombs constructed with vaulted roofs are found at S. Manno near Perugia (VI cent. B.C.), and in Chiusi and its territory (tombs « del Granduca », and « Vigna Grande », V cent. B.C.).

Late examples of this style exist at Bettona, near Perugia.

Sometimes the doors of the tomb (*Tarquinii*) and more rarely the interior (*Cerveteri*) are elaborately decorated with sculptured reliefs; in other instances, there are architectural decorations in the interior (*Cerveteri*) or on the exterior

BLERA - *Necropolis of rock-tombs.*

(*Faleri, Corchiano, Tuscania, Bieda, Musarna, Castel d'Asso, Norchia, Sovana*). At the two last-named sites there are rock-sepulchres with façades built in direct imitation of temples with sculptured pediments. Similar types of rock-tombs are found on the coast of Asia Minor.

At Orvieto there is a very interesting necropolis (VI-V cent. B.C.) laid out like a veritable « city of the dead » with parallel streets crossing one another at right angles and bordered closely with tombs of a uniform type.

But one of the greatest attractions of Etruscan tombs lies in their wealth of sepulchral paintings which are found almost exclusively at *Veii, Tarquinii, Orvieto* and *Chiusi*. They form a very special feature in the general history of Italic antiquities and we shall deal with them at greater length in the following chapter.

Sepulchral paintings [1]

In the *Campana* Tomb at *Veii* [2] we have the earliest specimens yet known to us (VII cent B.C.) of pictorial decoration in the dwellings of the dead: there are men and horses, wild beasts and grotesque animals, floral borders with palms and lotus flowers in yellow, grey and red on a blue ground. Six shields are painted on the wall of the inner chamber. None of the subjects have any reference to the world of the dead; they are only of ornamental value and we find the same style of art in tombs at *Cosa, Chiusi, Magliano* and *Cerveteri*.

Together with this generic kind of decoration, narrative paintings are found for the first time, in the *Tomb of the Bulls* at *Tarquinii* (middle VI cent. B.C.), where Achilles is represented lying in wait for Troilus near a fountain. It is a purely Greek subject, completely foreign to its surroundings, which shows how the Etruscans liked to beautify their tombs as though they were real dwelling-places, almost, it would seem, to perpetuate life in death.

---

[1] I have thought it advisable to speak at greater length of sepulchral paintings than of other aspects of Etruscan art, because while every guide-book is full of descriptions of objects preserved in Museums, it is generally difficult to find in them any synthetic description of the characteristics of wall-paintings in tombs which are comparatively rarely visited. But some of these more damaged pictures have now been removed from the tombs of Tarquinî and Orvieto and restored in Rome.

[2] It is well to bear in mind that the names given to tombs are in connection with some characteristic object either found or represented in them; or, more often, they are traditionally known by the name of the person who first discovered or described them.

8.

CERVÈTERI - *The tomb of the Bassorilievi or Stucchi* (Photo Brogi).

The decoration of the *Tomb of the Painted Reliefs* at *Cerveteri* (*Caere*) is particularly characteristic. It consists of subjects connected with daily life (hunting, fishing, kitchen utensils, etc.) carved in relief and coloured.

In a group of tombs dating from the middle of the VI century B.C. we notice a close connection with the paintings on Ionic vases and we also notice subjects having reference to their surroundings and fragmentary scenes that teach us something about Etruscan conceptions of death and eternity.

Such is, for example, the *Tomb of the Augurs* at *Tarquinii,* where scenes of sorrow for the dead are mingled with athletic contests and the *Pulcinella Tomb,* also at Tarquinii, so called from the figure of the Etruscan *Phersu,* who is fantastically dressed in a style not unlike the comic personage of Neapolitan drama; *Phersu,* attired as harlequin, is also depicted in the *Tomb of the Augurs,* taking part in a scene where a man, his head enveloped in a sack, is being savagely attacked by a dog, a brutal sport reminiscent of gladiatorial combats in Roman arenas. Athletic games accompanied by the sound of flutes also occur in the Tarquinian *Tomb of the Inscriptions* where there is a beautiful frieze of knights, dancers and fluteplayers. Dancing is a very favourite subject in Etruscan wall-paintings; we find it in several other tombs at Tarquinii, such as the *Tomb of the Dead Man* and the *Tomb of the Triclinium.* In this latter, the figures are represented with elegant dresses and in singularly graceful postures which are almost exaggerated in the female. The sex of the figure is distinguishable by its colour; that of the men is a deep red or brown, that of the women a pale yellow or creamy white, a conventional distinction which holds good in all Etruscan paintings.

Both for technique and composition, the *Tomb of the Baron* (at Tarquinii) deserves special mention. The scenes, which reveal Greek influence, either consist of almost motionless figures or of personages standing and conversing between horses decoratively disposed.

A period of Attic influence occurs about the middle of the V century B.C., an influence that can be traced, for example, in the profiles of the figures in the *Pulcinella Tomb* at *Tarquinii*. The *Tomba delle Bighe* or Chariot Tomb, also at Tarquinii, contains representations of funeral ceremonies, very valuable as a study of Etruscan customs, and scenes of athletic games taking place in the presence of numerous spectators. At Chiusi in the *Tomba della Scimmia* or Monkey-tomb, and the *Tomba del Colle Casuccini,* the paintings are executed in pale tints, almost like watercolours, and are painted directly on the stone, without any intermediate layer of stucco.

The Tarquinian *Tomb of the Leopards,* with scenes of couples seated together at a symposium; the *Tomb of the Funeral Couch* and the *Querciola Tomb* with various scenes taken from daily life, belong to this same period (middle of V cent. B.C.): The Tarquinian *Tomb of the Shields* and the *Tomb of the Ogre* are rather later (end of V cent.) and so is the *Tomb of the Velii* (*Golini*) near Orvieto, in all of which — as in the earlier *Tomb of the Old Men* at Tarquinii — are depicted couples male and female, seated or reclining at a banquet in attitudes that form interesting studies of Etruscan customs. At this period sepulchral

TARQUINIA - *Painting in the Tomb of the Triclinium (detail).*

The head of Proserpina (Phersipnei) in a picture in the tomb of the Ogre in Tarquinia (Photo Alinari).

inscriptions, with proper names, begin to be very frequent.

The beginning of the decadence of Etruscan power in the IV century coincides with a new style of sepulchral painting. The change is easily noticeable in the *Tomb of the Ogre* (Tarquinii) where besides the scene of the symposium, there is a hideous infernal demon with large wings and red snake-like locks. He has a pointed beard, a nose like an eagle's bill, and horse's ears; a huge snake springs from his shoulder and his buskins are laced with little serpents. He is garbed in a sleeveless tunic with a girdle and in his hand is a torch or hammer. His eyes shine with a sinister light in his bluish face.

Equally terrifying is the aspect of another demon, the horrible *Tuchulcha,* who appears in another scene in the same tomb. He has asses' ears, and two snakes bound round his brows and rearing themselves like horns above his forehead; a huge serpent is coiled round his left arm which is raised in a threatening manner above the head of the youthful Theseus who is seated, partly nude, upon a rock. Not less monstrous is the aspect of Charun armed with a hammer. From now onwards, the underworld of demons predominates in the paintings, an unmistakable sign of the terror that life beyond the grave inspired in the Etruscans of those days.

Another predominant element which also appears in the *Tomb of the Ogre* is taken from Greek mythology. Scenes and incidents from the lives of the gods and of Hellenic heroes are frequent, supplemented by long inscriptions with the Etruscan equivalents of Greek names. There is a characteristic tendency to reproduce scenes of cruelty as in the *François Tomb* at *Vulci* (2nd half of III cent. B.C.) where Achilles is seen cutting the throats of the Trojan captives, as a sacrifice to the shade of Patroclus. This is a very common subject in Etruscan art; we find it constantly on vases and sarcophagi. In the *François Tomb* the scene is completed by two purely Etruscan figures, Vanth, a benign female genius who watches over mortals when they die and *Charun,* the messenger of death.

In the same tomb we see *Mastarna* (better know by his Roman name of *Servius Tullius*) cutting the bonds of *Caeles Vibenna* and three groups of combatants, all of which are evidently historical allusions to Etruscan hegemony in Rome, during the period of the Kings.

Funeral processions accompanied by demons are found in the *Tomb of the Typhon* at Tarquinii, which dates from the middle of the IV century, B.C., perhaps even later; and in the *Tomb of the Cardinal* (beginning of III cent.) where some have thought that it was possible to detect — as also in other tombs of this late period — traces of Orphic-Pythagoric influences.

In tombs of the latest period we find the pictorial art fully developed, with an application of perspective, foreshortening and chiaroscuro, previously unknown.

Examples at Tarquinia following the discoveries of tombs that bring themselves into line with those already discovered, always complete a little more the artistic-historical picture of the great Tarquinian school (*Tombs delle Olimpiadi, delle Iscrizioni, della Nave,* etc.). But unfortunately the colours deteriorate rapidly, and one has to be quick to remove the pictures to be restored and kept in the museums.

SCULPTURE.

Sculpture, in Etruria, was largely an important art, first influenced by the East and afterwards by Greece, but Etruscan craftsmen managed to give their productions a personal touch which stamped them with a peculiarly national character. Their work is often good and sometimes excellent, full of life, and always expressive and true to nature.

Instead of marble, the noble medium of Greek art, the Etruscans made use of sandstone or tufa or even ordinary clay, out of which, with their marvellous skill, they created real masterpieces. From the primitive *canopi* or cinerary urns in the form of human busts, of the VII centenary B.C., from reliefs on doors of tombs (second half of VI cent.), we come to the *cippi* and coeval teramorphous figures placed at the entrance of tombs or temples, to the statuettes of *Chiusi, Narce* and *Falerii* and to the complicated reliefs of the end of the VI century B.C., inspired by Ionic influence, which decorate funeral couches and sarcophagi (*Chiusi, Cortona, Cerveteri*), their subjects being very similar to those described in the previous chapter on sepulchral paintings.

The *cippi* are peculiarly characteristic, and so are the *stelae* of which a typical archaic specimen was found at Vetulonia (VII cent. B.C.) inscribed with a « graffito » outline of a warrior, holding his two-edged axe. The *stelae* of Artiminio (middle of VI cent.) and Volterra (end of VI cent.) are both sculptured in relief with the figure of a warrior with a two-edged axe. The latter in addition bears a lance and the former a lance and a bow. *Stelae* have also been found at Londa, Antella, Fiesole and other neighbouring sites, not unsimilar to the type of the Felsinian stelae of a horse-shoe shape, decorated in bands, with borders ornamented with vine-shoots and ivy leaves.

A branch of sculpture in which Etruscan art excels is that of terracotta statuary, perfect in technique and individual in conception. The celebrated Apollo at Veii, the only quite perfect remaining figure of a group probably with Hercules and the gods which certainly existed in the interior of every temple together with a variety of votive gifts (images, objects, parts of the body, etc) offered to the deity. We should not forget that *Vulca,* a name that literary tradition has handed down to us as the author of the plastic statue of Jupiter in the Capitoline temple at Rome and of a statue of Hercules, was a Veientine. Mention must be made of the magnificent polychrome sarcophagi from *Caere,* with life-size figures of married couples reclining on the lids. The fictile decorations of temples have already been described on the p. 104.

The latest period of Etruscan art is marked by *sarcophagi* and *cinerary urns* adorned with fantastic animals and funeral reliefs of intricate scenes of combat taken from the epic and mythological cycles of Greece, such as the duel between Eteocles and Polynices: demons and Lase, the female genii of death, are generally added, and on the coffin lid is a realistic reproduction of the deceased, reclining and in the act of taking a libation or of accomplishing a last careful toilette for the supreme journey; the figure often holds a *patera* or a mirror, or else a roll inscribed with his or her name and qualities.

These sarcophagi and urns are found in terracotta (*Cerveteri*), in alabaster (*Volterra, Chiusi*), in *peperino* (*Tuscania*), in *nenfro* (*Tarquinia*), in fetid limestone (*Chiusi*), according to the natural material most easily obtained in each locality. Among the finest specimens are the polychrome sarcophagus of Torre S. Severo (red, yellow and blue), of the beginning of the III century B.C., decorated with the murder of the Trojan captives after the death of Patroclus, and with the sacrifice of Polixena on the tomb of Achilles; the polychrome sarcophagus of the *Magnate* at *Tarquinii,* the cinerary urns of *Chiusi,* and *Volterra* and, last in order of time, those of the hypogeum of the Volumni near *Perugia.*

* * *

The Etruscans have left incomparable masterpieces of *bronze* but the criterion that prevailed until a few years ago of attributing to Greek artists every object of artistic beauty yielded by the soil of ancient Etruria and of considering as purely Etruscan only such objects as were markedly inferior and provincial, caused the wonderful bronze statues of the *Capitoline Wolf* and the so-called « Brutus » in Rome and the *Chimaera* of Arezzo in Florence to be put down to Greek workmanship, though today nearly all the most competent judges of Etruscan art are unanimous in considering them both as the work of native artists. The celebrated *Wolf* undoubtedly reveals traces of Greek influence of the end of the VI century B.C., but in its every feature, in the realistic expression of the face glaring with

PALERMO, National Museum.
Sepulchral cippus from Chiusi.

FIESOLE, Museum. *Sepulchral stela from Travignoli.*

CASTIGLIONCELLO, Museum. *Cinerary urn.*

FLORENCE, Archaeological Museum.
Cinerary urn from Castiglioncello.

a threat of defence, not of offence, it is manifestly Etruscan. These characteristics are carried to the highest degree, perhaps almost to excess, in the *Chimaera,* which dates from about a century later. We seem to hear the roar of pain issuing from its open jaws as the monster writhes beneath the fatal wounds inflicted by the darts of Bellerophon.

Like the *Chimaera* it was found at Arezzo and was evidently made use of as a speaking oracle, as may be seen from the hole in the nape of the neck.

But on the threshold of Roman art, in the II century B.C., we have a genuine Etruscan work in the famous statue of the *Orator* (now in Florence) with his severe features and expression of speaking realism, discovered in the territory of Perugia, near Lake Trasimeno. From the long Etruscan inscription on the border of the *pallium,* we learn that this figure is the portrait of *Aulus Metellus.*

The statue of *Mars* (late work, found at Todi), now in the Vatican Museum, may also be excluded from authentic masterpieces of Etruscan art, owing to its somewhat theatrical pose, lack of definite expression and Phidias-like idealisation, it is more like Umbrian workmanship.

It is doubtful, on the other hand, whether the famous bronze statue of *Minerva* (I cent.) in Florence should be attributed to an Etruscan or a Roman artist, possibly to the latter.

Outstanding examples of the numerous minor bronzes — the *Tyrrhena sigilla* famous in antiquity for their artistic beauty — are certain small archaic figures of a youth worshipping (Isola di Fano), of maidens praying, of a warrior from Monte Falterona; the *Silenus* from Vetulonia, the *group of ploughmen* from Arezzo and Above all the tragically expressive *Ajax falling on his sword,* from Populonia, which some have wrongly attributed to a Greek artist.

To the latest phase of art belong statuettes of three nude boys, respectively from Cortona, Lake Thrasymene and Tar-

Particular of an urn in the Archaeological Museum at Florence.

9.

On the cover of an urn at Volterra.

quinii. Two of them are playing with a bird which shows
how a taste for such fanciful reproductions, common to
the Hellenistic age, had also penetrated into Etruria.

TOREUTICS.

The Etruscans produced a great number of works in
chiselled and hammered bronze, some of them of such
perfection in every minute detail as to rouse unbounded
admiration, even in comparison with Greek and Roman
masterpieces. Primitive urns of hammered plates nailed
together are followed by artistically decorated tripods, by
lebetes and *situlae,* the most important of which are the
exquisite specimens found at the Certosa near Bologna (end
of VI cent., B.C.) decorated with four bands of repoussé-
work. The finest of the chariots is the one found at Monte-
leone di Spoleto (VI cent. B.C.), though the marked Ionic
influence has caused it to be sometimes attributed to a
Greek artist. But the greatest wonder of all, of surpassing
beauty and elaboration, is the *Bronze Lamp* of Cortona (V
cent.), with its circle of sixteen smaller lamps decorated
alternately with a satyr and a syren; with its two concentric
bands, one filled with the wave-ornament and dolphins, the
other with animals fighting, while the centre contains a huge
Gorgon's face.

There are numerous specimens of censers and candelabra
and the slender-shafted *cottabys* used by the Etruscans in
a characteristic, convivial game, dating from the V-IV
centuries B.C. Then there are the beautiful hand-mirrors,

Particular of an urn at Siena.

decorated with repoussé or *graffito* work, marvellous
revelations of the careful and patient art of the Etruscan
toreutes who composed his delicate and graceful scenes
from subjects drawn from the legendary cycles of Greece,
to which he often added local elements, as may be seen
not only in strictly Etruscan productions but also in those
from the neighbouring Latin territories of *Latium* and
Praeneste. Graffito-work was generally the medium used

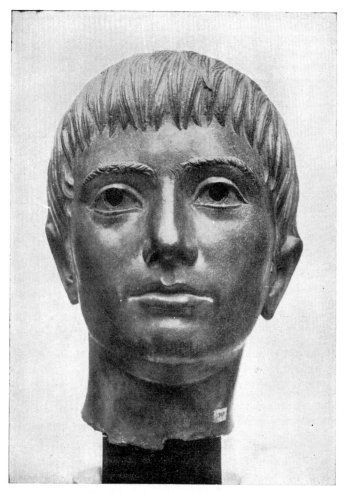

FLORENCE, Archaeological Museum.
The head of a young man. (Photo Alinari)

Rome, Museum of Valle Giulia. *Bronze bird from Volterra.*

on mirrors during nearly the whole period of development
of Etruscan art, from the VI to the II century B.C., though
with successive changes both in form and technique.

The Latin territory of *Praeneste* has also yielded numerous cistae, similarly decorated with graffiti, first oval
in shape, then cylindrical, with tiny figures or bronze groups
on the cover, forming the handle. The most beautiful *caist*
yet discovered is that known as the *Ficoronian* from Palestrina (IV cent. B.C.), with a scene from the legend of
Amycus, King of the Bebryces who was overcome by Pollux
during the expedition of the Argonauts.

POTTERY.

The extensive importation into Etruria of Greek pottery
which served as models for local manufacturers, makes it
sometimes difficult to decide to which of the two peoples
vases of a certain type are to be attributed, and this is
especially the case when the Etruscan products are obvious
imitations of Greek ware, as, for instance, the rich series
of hydriae from Caere, of an Ionic type, belonging to the
VI century B.C. Fortunately we are often helped by
inscriptions in one or other of the two languages. No doubts
can exist as to the origin of the characteristic *buccheri,*
or vases of dark clay, blackened by fumigation. Those of
the V century B.C. are found almost exclusively in the
neighbourhood of Chiusi. At first the bucchero vases are
thin, and decorated with oriental designs; during the VI-V
century they become more massive and are made in varied
and elegant forms, but towards the decline of Etruscan art,

A bronze lebetes from Vetulonia at Florence.

they are often of exaggerated proportions, with showy plastic decorations of doubtful taste and sometimes extravagant design, on the body, handles and cover of the vases.

Of importance from the second half of the VI century B.C., was a local production of « Ceretane » water vessels, almost certainly started by a Greek immagrant potter. At Cere was also produced the so called « bucchero rosso » stamped on the shiny surface.

Vulci also was a centre of vascular production; perhaps to it can be attributed the so called « pontici » vases of Ionic influence, that could also have been made at Tarquinia. As much uncertainty exists for the vases of the

FLORENCE, Archaeological Museum. *Bronze mirror from Bomarzo.*

ROMA, Museo privato Torlonia. *Bronze mirror with a mythical scene relative to the Trojan war.*

*Dish with the judgment of Paris, from Camucia (Cortona),
at Florence.*

PARIS, National Library. *Red figured crater with Admetus taking leave ol Alcestis between Charum (l.) and Tuchlcha (r.).*

« Painter of Micali », a school of potters flourishing between the end of the VI and the beginning of the V century B.C.

After the archaic pottery belonging to the group of Italo-geometric vases we come to vases decorated with black figures, imitations, that is, of the most ancient Greek technique, but with a characteristic brownish-coloured background, while the black pigment of the figures is opaque rather than shiny. This type has been found in various sites, but more especially in the district of Orvieto, where vases with a pale background decorated with funeral scenes have also been discovered. Vases with gold and silver reliefs, dating from the latter part of the III century B.C. were largely manufactured at Bolsena. Specimens of vases with red figures are not lacking and to Vulci above all are attributed the oldest and the most beautiful. Another productive centre in the second half of the V century B.C. is Volterra, especially large bowls with the high neck, also found at Perugia. There is a connection between Etruscan pottery and the vases of the Faliscan territory with light backgrounds, while these are again connected with the rich output of southern Italy, of a less sober type, with floral decorations.

JEWELLERY AND GLYPTICS.

The importance given by the Etruscans to personal adornment is revealed, not only in their mural paintings and statues, but in the extraordinary quantity of precious objects that have been excavated on every Etruscan site, most of them being in gold and gilt bronze. The earliest specimens are in granulated workmanship, later they are delicately frosted (*a pulviscolo*) or in filagree-work, and also to a large extent in enamelled glass (under the form of disks and polychrome beads), in amber, etc.

Rings, ear-rings and above all, fibulae, which we do not find after the V century B.C., are richly and exquisitely wrought and ornamented, and each period has its own typical forms.

The Etruscans were also very skilful in working precious stones. Up to the IV century B.C. scarabei of the Egyptian type and generally of red cornelian, were very common.

Their ivories, which are masterpieces of elaborate carving belong to the archaic period of the VII century. Especially beautiful is the ivory cup from Chiusi, carved with bands of reliefs representing scenes from the Greek heroic cycle, dealing with the story of Ulysses. The ivory carvings of Prenaeste and Caere are also very fine.

TABLE OF CONTENTS

A SHORT SUMMARY OF THE HISTORY, CIVILISATION, LANGUAGE AND ART OF THE ETRUSCANS

HISTORY AND CIVILISATION:

Finito di stampare a Firenze con i tipi della tipolitografia F.lli Linari - giugno 1968